T
SACRED MAGICIAN

a ceremonial diary

William Bloom

GOTHIC IMAGE PUBLICATIONS

This Edition first published 1992 by
Gothic Image Publications
7 High Street, Glastonbury, Somerset BA6 9DP

The extracts from
The Book of the Sacred Magic of Abramelin the Mage
are reproduced unaltered from the second edition of the work
which was published by John M. Watkins, London, in 1900.
A full reproduction is available published by Dover Books,
New York 1975.

Cover artwork by Peter Woodcock

Text design and production by
Mentor DTP
Bruton, Somerset

A catalogue record for this book is available
from the British Library

Printed and bound in Great Britain

"...devoutly and with boldness ye shall invoke the Name of the Lord, thanking Him for all the grace which He hath given and granted unto you from your infancy until now; then with humility shall ye humble yourselves unto Him, and confess unto Him entirely all your sins; supplicating Him to be willing to pardon you and remit them. Ye shall also supplicate Him that in the time to come He may be willing and pleased to regard you with pity and grant you His grace and goodness to send unto you His Holy Angel, who shall serve unto you as a Guide, and lead you ever in His Holy Way and Will..."

William Bloom is a writer, lecturer, counseller and organiser whose work is dedicated to integrating the wisdom and techniques of the mystery traditions into a relevant approach to contemporary social and personal transformation. He has a doctorate in Psychology from the London School of Economics. He is a founding director of Alternatives of St James's, and is closely involved with the educational programme of the Findhorn Foundation.

By the same author:
Meditation in a Changing World
Devas, Fairies and Angels,
Sacred Times
The New Age
The Seeker's Guide

Acknowledgements

This book is the diary that I kept during a six month magical ritual known as *The Sacred Magic of Abramelin the Mage*. The diary was originally published in 1976 under a pseudonym because I felt unable at that time to deal with any of the requests or enquiries that might have then been directed to me. Twenty years on I have integrated most of the experience, perhaps am wiser and have received many requests to republish it under my own name.

In this edition I have also included an Introduction and Epilogue, notes throughout the text, as well as reproductions from the instructions of *The Sacred Magic* itself. The Introduction explains why I went into the ceremony in the first place and the Epilogue describes what happened to me afterwards.

My thanks to Palden Jenkins and Andrew Hill for their editorial help.

My deep appreciation to Frances Howard-Gordon and Jamie George for their support and love at many levels.

And, finally, a loving thank you to Sabrina for her wisdom, insight and inspiration.

CONTENTS

for
James Bloom

INTRODUCTION

In the Autumn of 1972 I left my career as a London publisher and novelist to travel south to Morocco in order to perform an intense six month ritual of ceremonial magic, the climax of which is communication with one's Holy Guardian Angel.

I was twenty-five years old and had spent three years intensely reading mystical, occult and spiritual literature. I had first come across this literature when, as a commissioning editor in a London publishing house, someone had submitted to me a manuscript on out-of-the-body experiences. Until that point in time I had been an active and aggressive cynic about spirituality, but there was something about the book which rang instinctive bells of truth within me. I began then to read two or three mystic and occult books a week, beginning with Sufi literature, moving eastwards into Buddhist and yogic teachings, and then returning westwards into the Christian, gnostic, kabbalistic and western mystery tradition in general. After these three years of reading, meditating, trying various exercises, but never joining a group or seeking a guru, I reached a point where reading and the occasional exercise were no longer enough. I had an overwhelming instinct fully to enter the world about which I was reading.

It was then that I came across a book that is famous in the western magical tradition, *The Book of the Sacred Magic of Abramelin the Mage*. Translated by S.L. MacGregor Mathers from a fifteenth century manuscript held in the Bibliotheque de l'Arsenal in Paris, the book describes a six month ritual of ceremonial magic, the culmination of which is full conversation with one's Holy Guardian Angel and then the conjuration and subjection of evil spirits. I was impressed by its clarity of purpose and the purity of its technique.

(I reproduce towards the front of this book a facsimile of the relevant sections from the 1900 edition of *The Book of the Sacred Magic*. Then, within the Diary itself, I refer readers back to the relevant passages in this facsimile.)

The ritual, described in great detail in *The Book of the Sacred Magic*, lasts six months and in order to pursue it, the ritualist needs to be in a place that will be undisturbed and where he can build an oratory or small chapel. In this oratory he needs a small altar, an oil lamp, a charcoal incense burner and a corner covered with sand from a river. He is also required to make special robes, holy oil and incense, and to cut an almond shoot to act as his wand. For six months, starting at Easter, the ritualist prays, with increasing intensity, and for increasingly long periods, that his sins be forgiven and that, now forgiven, he will be granted full communication with his Holy Guardian Angel. Having been granted this full conversation he is then allowed to summon up the forces of evil, devils and demons. Supported by his Holy Guardian Angel and working on behalf of God and the Forces of Light, he summons these demons by name and has them pledge obedience to him should he ever wish or need to control them.

When I committed myself to this six month ritual my attitude was dualistic. On one side I approached it purely from a psychological perspective. On the other I approached it with the full commitment of a devoted mystic. I thought that I was about to explore two landscapes.

The first landscape was within my own psyche where I would reveal to myself, under the guise of the Holy Guardian Angel, a core aspect of my true self. From this perspective, the Holy Guardian Angel was a metaphor for my own soul, my own eternal essence. The demons and devils, then, were *shadow* aspects of my own psyche which under normal circumstances I would not have the courage or the psychological technology to encounter. I expected to take my awareness into the realm of what Jung described as the collective unconscious where I would meet archetypal forms belonging to the racial or genetic memory of all women and men. The Holy Guardian Angel would be an archetypal concept, or reality, held within the collective psyche of humanity; as also would be the devils and demons.

But, at the same time, I thought that I was also about to explore a second landscape: a world of spiritual realities normally unperceived by our five senses. In this world there were real angels and real demons. I was prepared to think this because I had many times in my life, since early childhood, experienced atmospheres and presences, some beautiful and ecstatic, others spooky and frightening. These experiences had been too frequent and too substantial for my mind to reject. Equally, all the mystical and esoteric books I read, regardless of creed or culture, spoke clearly and explicitly about this invisible world of energies, vibrations and consciousnesses. I could not dismiss this vast wealth of authoritative and corroborating literature.

To understand my diary better I am certain that the reader needs to be more familiar with the young man who went into that ceremony.

I had been brought up by two parents who were intellectual humanists and I had been educated in the mainstream British private school tradition. From an early age – I remember them clearly from the age of five – I had experiences of another reality but, like many children, kept them to myself. I kept quiet about them because these experiences were in direct conflict with the essence of the worldview that was parenting and educating me. I was a shy and well-behaved infant, but as I grew older I became increasingly cynical and increasingly aggressive. I was usually too timid to let this aggression surface openly, but often it emerged as mockery or as an intense intellectual competitiveness.

As I moved into my twenties my cynicism and aggression became increasingly focused on political and cultural targets. I aligned myself with the radical and occasionally violent factions of the flower-power and counter-culture movement of the 1960s. Looking back I fully understand why this movement suited me so well. Counter-culture was politically radical, but it was also in conflict with the mainstream psychological and philosophical understanding of the world and of reality. Through its psychedelic experiences and its exploration of eastern and shamanic techniques for altering consciousness, counter-culture supported the notion of an invisible reality; and through its alignment with surrealism and situationism it also actively sought to create *events* which altered perspective and experience.

In many ways the tension within me – between my mainstream education and my instinct for the mystical, between my aggression and my idealism, further driven by a compulsive personality – was unbearable. I remember for a while in my early twenties holding off waves of confusion, of alienation and of total identity crisis. When I was twenty-two and had my first novel published, with all the trappings of a publisher's important launch, followed by much press coverage and lead reviews in the quality press – a dream for the first publication of a young novelist – I felt only meaninglessness. As I became increasingly successful as a writer and a publisher, this sense of meaninglessness grew.

I then had two extraordinary meetings with older men which helped to heal me. It is important in the context of this diary to write about my encounter with these two men. I look back on my pursuit of the Abramelin Ceremony as a rite of passage into a sacred dimension or as what is called in some native peoples' traditions a 'vision quest.' And, as I look back, I see these two older men giving me their blessing and their power for the journey. Perhaps I would have gone ahead without my experience of them, but Lord knows how I would have fared.

I also write about them because I am becoming increasingly aware of a terrible injury to our modern culture. This injury is caused by the fact that so many millions of us grow up without ever receiving the true attention, the true love, the true enthusiasm and affection of an older wiser woman or man. This blessing from our elders has in our society become coldly institutionalised into gradings and marks at the end of a class, into certificates and awards, into promotion within a bureaucracy, into increased salaries and wages – but hardly ever do we receive the deep blessing of an enthusing elder. We need all of us to be welcomed, received and warmly given space in our cultures. Alienation is built into our cultural structures if there is no safe reception for us. We need, I feel, desperately to regain this most important trans- action between the generations. I encourage you to enthuse and love your younger friends, to create a powerful path for their gifts into the future.

I also write about these two men because neither of them was a magician or an obvious mystical guru, even though they were both truly witch-doctors, one a psychoanalyst and the other a novelist.

The first encounter was with the American writer, James Baldwin, who after reading my second novel, asked to meet me. We met at a private literary dinner in London and immediately went into deep conversation and rapport. A few friends said, cynically, that I was attractive and that Jimmy, who was gay, had fallen in love with me; that was not my experience. We spent a weekend together in which he gave me his total adoring attention, never moving into physical sexuality. He whispered his love to me and he spoke his love to me in the prose that made him so powerful a writer. He said he would be prepared to die for me, that I was one of the great souls, that he and I were two of the last niggers left, that if we slept in the ghetto he would place his body between mine and the window to save me from the assassin's bullet. I told him I thought I was mad and alone; and he embraced me and said welcome, brother. We rode around London together on my motorbike, his arms around me, his head resting against my back. Over and over again, he told me that I was not alone, that there were men who could understand my soul and that I was all right, that I was fine and wonderful, that I was loved and respected.

I could not reject the intensity of his communication. It was not so much his words into my mind, but his total attention touching the whole of my personality and identity. For three days I experienced a great man's love, adoration and respect – and I drank it in at this oasis in my confused life. He returned to his home in southern France and never wrote to me. I think that the episode in some strange way hurt him, that he had made a sacrifice of some part of himself to heal me. I wrote to thank him and to continue the relationship in a calmer way, but there was only silence. I think that he felt that he had made a fool of himself.

Mystically I feel that my soul had called his soul in to help me. I was an intense, aggressive and confused psyche, and only the kind of power which he indeed delivered could touch me.

I had another love affair, of a completely different sort and rhythm, with my psychoanalyst, Edward Glover. My father, an eclectic Freudian psychiatrist, had always said to me that if ever I wanted full psychoanalysis he would set up the introductions. At twenty-two, during a temporary break from Frances, I found that I could not make love adequately. (I soon discovered that I did not have a problem and that one-night stands were simply not for me.) At the same time, I was fully aware that my increasing interest in the occult and mystical could be interpreted, in a Freudian mode, as a form of escapism or psychic compensation. My temporary sexual anxiety and awareness of the Freudian-materialistic critique of my mysticism led me into analysis.

Edward Glover was eighty-one years old when I first saw him. He was one of the founders of the psychoanalytic school in Britain and had himself known Freud; his own books were important texts and he had a powerful reputation. During the course of my psychoanalysis, I became his last analysand and we moved our sessions from his consulting rooms to his home in Marylebone where he was still looking after his own daughter, who had Downs Syndrome. His books were rigorous and intellectually aggressive, but in his psychoanalytic practice he was wry, gentle and twinkly, his voice conveying his comments in an amused but concerned Scottish drawl. He was the first man I had met who could easily and calmly point a finger at my bullshit and inconsistencies; his mind was faster and cannier than mine and I loved him for it. He was bald and looked very sweet, and smoked many cigarettes; I also smoked at the time and we developed a ritual of smoking each other's cigarettes alternately.

For the first year and a half he gave me the gift of just allowing me to talk and to talk and to talk, occasionally poking in a comment about an inconsistency or contradiction. Then our sessions began to develop into conversations and he gave me the gift of talking to me, of sharing his own thoughts and ponderings, thus breaking all the rules of classical psychoanalysis. I do not know whether he had done this with his other analysands. He told me something about his own analysis and training. Moreover he stopped charging me for the sessions – both a practical and symbolic gesture.

For eighteen months we talked. He gave me trust and, like James Baldwin, he also dared to make extravagant and romantic statements which sank deeply into my heart, giving me a foundation of confidence from which to be fully present. Once he said to me with a chuckle, "Ah, William, you and I are probably the last two analysts alive that I would trust." What a gift to an insecure young person. Together we decided that I was not an emotional cripple and that, therefore, my interest in mysticism and the occult had some sensible basis to it. He was not sure what this basis was, but he was open to it. I had his trust rather than my father's and society's suspicion.

Three weeks before I was due to go to Morocco we brought our relationship to an end. It was a poignant moment and for the first time we touched and hugged, two men in London unversed in how to hold another man. He then died a week later. I went to his funeral in the crematorium and I think I was the only person there who cried. And I think I was the only person there who prayed. We had helped prepare each other for our voyages.

My gratitude to both men flows over, I hope, into my other relationships.

So I knew when I was twenty-four that I had to reorient my life completely; I knew that I needed to face myself; I knew that I needed fully to experience the world of the occult and the mystic. Only the intensity of such a procedure as the Abramelin Operation – 'Operation' being a word used in the original manuscript to refer to the ceremony – would work for me. Then and now, I was not interested in the phenomena available through such an act of ritual magic; I was interested in the process through which it would take me.

I left London in the Autumn of 1972 accompanied by Frances Howard-Gordon; she and I had been together since we were fifteen and sixteen years old. She had been working as a director in BBC television current affairs, but was sacked in 1971 as part of a purge of left-wing and feminist radicals. She is a fiery, beautiful and creative woman, who has always had her own interest in the psychedelic and the mystical. We had also always enjoyed adventures and this voyage to Morocco, and then into worlds invisible and uncharted, was not to be missed by her. She was ready for a change from the western urban and media life style.

I gradually brought my publishing and community politics activities to an end. I organised a small book contract for some paperback mystical thrillers which would provide income to cover the trip. (I had four of these thrillers published under the pseudonym of W.W. Their hero was an Asian prince and occultist sent by the invisible inner government of the world to balance out evil!) Morocco was chosen as the location of the ceremony for several reasons: I had twice previously visited there and had a sense of the country. It was inexpensive. It still had an active magical tradition and respect for spiritual practice. I also simply had a deep intuition that we would find the appropriate location there, somewhere in the High Atlas Mountains south of Marrakesh and north of the Sahara.

We set off in the Autumn of 1971 in a Volkswagen camping van, drove across France and Spain, and then took the ferry across the Straights of Gibraltar. We had several fairly bizarre adventures as we travelled around Morocco looking for our location. These adventures included: our VW's engine collapsing on the busiest motorway into Casablanca and our sleeping in the van for several nights parked in between two brothels; a stay in the village of musicians where they still conduct a six thousand year old elaborate musical invocation and then channelling of Pan; and the transportation of a van full of elderly female Muslim pilgrims across Morocco to the airport where they took the plane to Mecca for the annual Haj pilgrimage.

Finally, after much travelling and exploration, we found the perfect location. I do not want to identify the exact village and valley because the place was unspoilt by tourists and deserves to remain so. Six thousand feet up in the High Atlas mountains, close to Mount Toupkal, the highest mountain in north Africa, separated by two miles and a river from the nearest tarmacked road, our house had been built as a French colonial boar-hunting lodge. It consisted of three rooms in a row with a veranda and twenty yards from it was a small sun terrace sitting on its own. Its water was brought down from a nearby well. The house belonged to the local cement factory owner whom we met through the local bus owner – Frances was always extraordinary at making connections – and the owner was happy to see it occupied and to receive rent. I was simply an English writer seeking quiet.

The sun terrace was obviously where I could build the oratory. We moved into the house in November 1972 and passed through a winter which included four feet of snow. I built the oratory and the altar, made the holy perfume and the oil, and cut my wand. Frances made my ceremonial robes. On the day of the Spring Equinox 1973 I began the Operation.

Rereading the Diary, before publishing it as this book, it was clear that certain parts of it needed clarifying as I had not written the Diary for publication. The manuscript, therefore, was given to two friends and editors for their suggestions and both made very useful comments, many of which have been incorporated. One of them, however, wanted a complete description of how Frances and I were living day-by-day and a blow-by-blow psychological explanation of what I was going through. It was suggested, for example, that without more explanatory notes I would come over as earnest, pompous and a bit of a chauvinist; but the truth is that I *was* all of those things at the time. Equally, the other wanted every single reference to my spiritual and occult experiences explained – but to attempt to explain blow-by-blow the different energies and impressions I experienced would be to suggest far greater knowledge and control than I actually possessed. It was all very intense and the truth is that I was barely sane through the whole event. As I state repeatedly in the Diary, I did not fully understand what was happening. I, therefore, decided not to incorporate all their suggestions, for then there would be more notes than Diary. The Diary would also lose its mystery if everything were explained. The reader needs also to remember that it was not written for publication, but was simply my own journal, often written in haste, often written in confusion.

In particular, in retrospect, I cannot easily explain how a radical young novelist, publisher and community activist became – the moment that I knelt for the first time in the Oratory I had built – the intense and psychologically self-flagellatory Judaeo-Christian mystic. But when you read the extracts from the careful instructions of *The Book of the Sacred Magic* you will see explicit directions to the magician to humble himself and acknowledge his sins before God. From one perspective this is simply a psychological technique to keep the unruly ego in order. From another occult perspective, to confess humbly every day cleanses the energy of the whole personality and, over six months, builds up a protective force that allows the magician successfully to complete the whole ceremony. So, when I write repeatedly in the Diary about my 'wormhood' it is not a false humility; it is a genuine aspect of my being fully in the spirit of the Operation. And certainly, as I felt my inner resistance to the daily disciplines, I did genuinely feel myself to be a worm, especially in relation to the transcendent states of consciousness I was also experiencing. This is an inner duality about which I am kinder to myself today. Equally, once I had started the Sacred Magic it felt as if I had launched myself into a sacred drama, a ritual of mystery, with its own distinct flavour and dynamic; I had no choice but to surrender myself completely to its cultural integrity.

I need to describe more fully in this introduction our physical location and our daily routine, especially so that Frances does not disappear as some submissive and oppressed image which would be the very opposite of who she is and what she did. Throughout the six month period, although acutely aware and supportive of what I was doing, Frances led her own independent life. We were living in a wonderful mountain valley landscape and, no longer in the centre of London, there were always many things to do and to observe. There were orange and almond trees in our garden, and a very large vegetable patch tended by a local Berber and his family. Eagles would fly over us low enough so that we could feel the air from the beat of their wings and flocks of storks would stop in our garden when it was being watered. Snakes and lizards lived and sunbathed around us. And when it was very wet, hundreds of toads from the river would travel the half mile up the slope of the valley to surround our house and create an obstacle course for humans at night. There were very beautiful walks in all directions and there were relationships to keep up with the local people such as the post master, the chief of police and so on. Frances and I had been released for the first time from urban life into rural bliss.

Where we lived was extraordinarily beautiful. The people were open, spiritual and friendly. Physically and socially, we were in heaven.

We drove down into Marrakesh once a week to do the shopping and we took it in turns to cook. Frances had many books to read and was also working on her own writing. We also had occasional visitors, mentioned in the Diary, and Frances spent time with them exploring the local area. From these visitors' perspective and from the perspective of the locals, I appeared to be an introspective and antisocial writer who liked praying in his home-built chapel. Frances, however, was outgoing and amiable, and made us acceptable. She was also a strong magical worker in her own right and I was always aware and grateful for her support; I knew then, as I still do, that there are few women, or men, strong enough or generous enough to accompany me through such a time.

THE BOOK

OF THE

SACRED MAGIC

OF ABRAMELIN THE MAGE,

AS DELIVERED BY ABRAHAM THE JEW UNTO HIS SON LAMECH, A.D. 1458.

Translated from the Original Hebrew into the French, and now rendered from the latter language into English. From a unique and valuable MS. in the "Bibliothèque de l'Arsenal" at Paris.

BY

S. L. MAC GREGOR MATHERS,

Author of "The Kabbalah Unveiled," "The Key of Solomon," "The Tarot," etc.

THE SEVENTH CHAPTER.

REGARDING WHAT IT IS NECESSARY TO ACCOMPLISH DURING THE FIRST TWO MOONS OF THE BEGINNING OF THIS VERITABLE AND SACRED MAGIC.

E who commenceth this Operation should consider with care that which we have before said, and should pay attention unto that which followeth ; and the thing being of importance, I shall leave alone for the present all other considerations, so that we may begin with the Operation which we should perform on the first morning after the celebration of the Feast of Easter (or Passover).

Firstly : Having carefully washed one's whole body and having put on fresh clothing : precisely a quarter of an hour before Sunrise ye shall enter into your Oratory, open the window, and place yourselves upon your knees before the Altar, turning your faces towards the window ; and devoutly and with boldness ye shall invoke the Name of the Lord, thanking Him for all the grace which He hath given and granted unto you from your infancy until now ; then with humility shall ye humble yourselves unto Him, and confess unto Him entirely all your sins ; supplicating Him to be willing to pardon you and remit them. Ye shall also supplicate Him that in the time to come He may be willing and pleased to regard you with pity and grant you His grace and goodness to send unto you His Holy Angel, who shall serve unto you as a Guide, and lead you ever in His Holy Way and Will ; so that ye fall not into sin through inadvertence, through ignorance, or through human frailty.

In this manner shall ye commence your Oration, and continue thus every morning during the first two Moons or Months.

Meseemeth here that now some may say : " Where-fore dost thou not write down the words or form of prayer the which I should employ, seeing that, as for me, I am neither sufficiently learned, nor devout, nor wise ? "

Know ye that although in the beginning your prayer be but feeble, it will suffice, provided that ye understand how to demand the Grace of the Lord with love and a true heart, whence it must be that such a prayer cometh forth. Also it serveth nothing to speak without devotion, without attention, and without intelligence ; nor yet to pronounce it with the mouth alone, without a true intent ; nor yet to read it as do the ignorant and the impious. But it is absolutely necessary that your prayer should issue from the midst of your heart, because simply setting down prayers in writing, the hearing of them will in no way explain unto you how really to pray.* This is the reason that I have not wished to give unto you any special form of prayers and orations, so that ye yourselves may learn from and of yourselves how to pray, and how to invoke the Holy Name of God, our Lord ; and for that reason I have not been willing that ye should rely upon *me* in order to pray. Ye have the Holy and Sacred Scripture, the which is filled with very beautiful and potent prayers and actions of grace. Study then herein, and learn herefrom, and ye shall have no lack of instruc-tions how to pray with fruit. And although in the commencement your prayer may be weak, it sufficeth that your heart be true and loyal towards God, Who little by little will kindle in you His Holy Spirit, Who will so teach you and enlighten your Spirit, that ye shall both know and have the power to pray.

When ye shall have performed your orations, close

* This is the great point to be studied in all Magical Operations soever, and unless the whole heart and soul and faith go with the ceremony, there can be no reliable result produced.

the window, and go forth from the Oratory ; so that no
one may be able therein to enter ; and ye shall not yourselves enter again until the evening when the Sun shall
be set.   Then shall ye enter therein afresh, and shall
perform your prayers in the same manner as in the
morning.

For the rest, ye shall govern yourselves each day as
I shall tell you in the following instructions.

Concerning the Bed Chamber and the Oratory, and
how they should be arranged, I will tell hereafter in the
Eleventh Chapter.*

It is requisite that ye shall have a Bed Chamber near
the Oratory or else your ordinary habitation, which it is
necessary first to thoroughly clean out and perfume, and
see that the Bed be both new and clean.   Your whole
attention must be given to purity in all things ; because
the Lord hath in abomination all that is impure.   You
shall sleep in this said Chamber, and you shall continue
therein during the day, there transacting the matters
which belong unto your business ; and those which you
can dispense with, leave alone.   You may sleep with
your Wife in the bed when she is pure and clean ; but
when she hath her monthly courses you shall not allow her
to enter the bed, nor even the Chamber.   Every Sabbath-
eve it is necessary to change the sheets of the bed, and all
the linen.   Every Saturday you shall perfume the Chamber.
And ye shall not allow any dog, cat, or other animal
to enter into nor dwell therein ; so that they may in no
way be able to render it unclean.   As regardeth the
matrimonial obligation, it is chastity, and the duty that
of engendering children ; but the whole should be done
in the Fear of God, and, above all things, in such case see
that your Wife be not impure.   But during the following
four Moons ye shall flee sexual intercourse as ye would

* The title of the Eleventh Chapter of the Second Book is :
"Concerning the Selection of the Place".

the Plague. Even if ye have children, endeavour to send them away unto another place before (commencing the Operation), so that they may not be an hindrance from being about you ; except the eldest-born of the family, and infants at the breast.

As regardeth the regimen of your life and actions, ye shall have regard unto your status and condition. If you be your own Master, as far as lieth in your power, free yourself from all your business, and quit all mundane and vain company and conversation ; leading a life tranquil, solitary and honest. If aforetime you have been a wicked, debauched, avaricious, luxurious and proud man, leave and flee from all these Vices. Consider that this was one of the principal reasons why ABRAHAM, MOSES, DAVID, ELIJAH, JOHN, and other holy men retired into desert places, until that they had acquired this Holy Science and Magic ; because where there are many people, many scandals do arise ; and where scandal is, Sin cometh ; the which at length offendeth and driveth away the Angel of God, and the Way which leadeth unto Wisdom becometh closed unto ye. Fly as far as you can the conversation of men, and especially of such as in the past have been the companions of your debauches ; or who have led you into sin. Ye shall therefore seek retirement as far as possible ; until that ye shall have received that Grace of the Lord which ye ask. But a Domestic Servant* who is compelled to serve a Master cannot well have these conveniences (for working and performing the Operation).

Take well heed in treating of business, in selling or buying, that it shall be requisite that you never give way unto anger, but be modest and patient in your actions.

You shall set apart two hours each day after having dined, during the which you shall read with care the Holy Scripture and other Holy Books, because they will

---

* Meaning in the case where the Aspirant unto the Sacred Magic is a Servant actually then serving a Master.

teach you to be good at praying, and how to fear the Lord ; and thus day by day shall ye better know your Creator. The other exercises which be free and permitted unto you, are hereafter set forth and principally in the Eleventh Chapter.

As for eating, drinking and sleeping, such should be in moderation and never superfluous. It is especially necessary to shun drunkenness, and flee public dinners. Content yourself with eating at your own house, with your family, in the peace and quiet which God hath granted unto you. You should never sleep during the day, but you may in the morning, for after that you have performed your devotions you may if you wish again go to bed to rest yourself. And if it happeneth by chance that you do not rise sufficiently early, that is to say before sunrise, it doth not greatly matter (provided that it be not done of evil intent), and you shall perform your ordinary morning prayer ;* but you should not accustom yourself to be slothful, it being always better to pray unto God at an early hour.

CONCERNING CLOTHING AND FAMILY.

Your dress should be clean but moderate, and according to custom. Flee all vanity. You shall have two dresses, in order that you may be able to change them ; and you shall change them the eve of each Sabbath, wearing the one one week, and the other the next ; brushing and perfuming them always beforehand.

As for that which regardeth the family, the fewer in

---

* The object of most of these instructions is of course to keep the Astral Sphere of the Aspirant free from evil influences, and accustom him to pure and holy thoughts and to the exercise of Will power and Self-control. The student of the Indian Tatwas will know the value of active meditation at Sunrise because that moment is the Akâsic commencement of the Tatwic course in the day, and of the power of the Swara.

number, the better ; also act so that the servants may be modest and tranquil. All these pieces of advice be principal points which it is well to observe. As for the rest, you have only to keep before your eyes the Tables of the Law during all this time, and also afterwards ; because these Tables should be the rule of your life.

Let your hand be ever ready to give alms and other benefits to your neighbour ; and let your heart be ever open unto the poor, whom God so loveth that one cannot express the same.

And in the case that during this period you should be attacked by some illness, which would not permit you to go unto the Oratory, this need not oblige you to abandon your enterprise at once ; but you should govern yourself to the best of your ability ; and in such case you shall perform your orations in your bed, entreating God to restore you to health, so that you may be enabled to continue your undertaking, and make the sacrifices which be due, and so with the greater strength be able to work to obtain His Wisdom.

And this is all that we should do and observe during these two Moons.

THE EIGHTH CHAPTER.

CONCERNING THE TWO SECOND MOONS.

THE two first Moons being finished ; the two second Moons follow, during the which ye shall make your prayer, morning and evening at the hour accustomed ; but before entering into the Oratory ye shall wash your hands and face thoroughly with pure water. And you shall prolong your prayer with the greatest possible affection, devotion and submission ; humbly entreating the Lord God that He would deign to command His Holy

70   THE BOOK OF THE SACRED MAGIC

Angels to lead you in the True Way, and Wisdom, and Knowledge, by studying the which assiduously in the Sacred Writings there will arise more and more (Wisdom) in your heart.

The use of the rights of Marriage is permitted, but should scarcely if at all be made use of (during this period).

You shall also wash your whole body every Sabbath Eve.

As to what regardeth commerce and manner of living, I have already given unto you sufficient instruction.

Only it is absolutely necessary to retire from the world and seek retreat ; and ye shall lengthen your prayers to the utmost of your ability.

As for eating, drinking and clothing, ye shall govern yourselves in exactly the same manner as in the two first Moons ; except that ye shall fast (the Qabalistical fast) every Sabbath Eve.

NOTE WELL : The Sabbath is for the Jews, who are accustomed to observe the same every Saturday, but for Christians the Sabbath is the Sunday, and they* ought to consider the Saturday as its Eve.

THE NINTH CHAPTER.

CONCERNING THE TWO LAST MOONS WHICH MUST BE THUS COMMENCED.

ORNING and Noon ye shall wash your hands and your face on entering the Oratory ;† and firstly ye shall make Confession of all your sins ; after this, with a very ardent prayer, ye shall entreat the

---

* *I.e.*, the Christians.

† This probably means in the bed-chamber *before entering* the Oratory.

Lord to accord unto you this particular grace, which is, that you may enjoy and be able to endure * the presence and conversation of His Holy Angels, and that He may deign by their intermission to grant unto you the Secret Wisdom, so that you may be able to have dominion over the Spirits and over all creatures.

Ye shall do this same at midday before dining, and also in the evening ; so that during these two last Moons ye shall perform the prayer three times a day, and during this time ye shall ever keep the Perfume upon the Altar. Also towards the end of your Oration, ye shall pray unto the Holy Angels, supplicating them to bear your sacrifice before the Face of God, in order to intercede for you, and that they shall assist you in all your operations during these two Moons.

The man who is his own master † shall leave all business alone, except works of charity towards his neighbour. You shall shun all society except that of your Wife and of your Servants. Ye shall employ the greatest part of your time in speaking of the Law of God, and in reading such works as treat wisely thereof ; so that your eyes may be opened unto that which from past time even unto the present ye have not as yet seen, nor thought of, nor believed.

Every Sabbath Eve shall ye fast, and wash your whole body, and change your garment.

Furthermore, ye shall have a Vest and Tunic of linen, which ye shall put on every time that ye enter into the Oratory, before ye commence to put the Perfume in the Censer, as I shall tell ye more fully hereafter

Also ye shall have a basket or other convenient vessel of copper filled with Charcoal to put inside the Censer when necessary, and which ye can take outside the Ora-

---

* *Que vous puissiez jouir et résister à la présence*, etc.
† *I.e.*, independent.

tory, because the Censer itself should never be taken away from the place.   Note well that after having performed your prayer, you ought to take it* out of the Oratory, especially during the Two last Moons, and ye should inter it in a place which cannot well be made unclean, such as a garden.

THE TENTH CHAPTER.

CONCERNING WHAT THINGS A MAN MAY LEARN AND STUDY DURING THESE TWO MOONS.

ALTHOUGH the best counsel which I can give is that a man should go into retirement in some desert or solitude, until the time of the Six Moons destined unto this Operation be fulfilled, and that he shall have obtained that which he wisheth ; as the Ancients used to do ; nevertheless now this is hardly possible ; and we must accommodate ourselves unto the era (in which we live) ; and being unable to carry it out in one way, we should endeavour to do so in another ; and attach ourselves only unto Divine Things.

But there be certain who cannot even do this thoroughly, notwithstanding they may honestly wish the same ; and this because of their divers employments and positions which will not permit them to act in accordance with their desires, so that they are compelled to carry on their worldly occupations.

In order then that such may know what occupations and business they can follow out without prejudice to this Operation, I will here state the same in few words.

We may then exercise the profession of Medicine, and all arts connected with the same ; and we may per-

---

* *I.e.*, the ashes of the charcoal and incense.

form all operations which tend unto charity and mercy towards our neighbour purely and simply. As for what concerneth the liberal arts ye may interest yourselves in Astronomy, etc., but flee all arts and operations which have the least tincture of Magic and Sorcery, seeing that we must not confound together God and Belial : God wisheth to be alone ; unto Him pertain all honour and glory. All the above matters are however permitted during the two first and the two second Moons.

You may walk in a garden for recreation ; but you shall do no servile work ; and amidst the flowers and the fruits you can also meditate upon the greatness* of God. But during the two third and last Moons ye shall quit every other matter only permitting your recreation to consist in things Spiritual and Divine. If ye wish to be participators in the Conversation of the Angels, and in the Divine Wisdom, lay aside all indiscreet † things, and regard it as a pleasure when ye can spare two or three hours to study the Holy Scripture, because hencefrom ye shall derive incredible profit ; and even the less ye are learned, so much the more will ye become wise and clever. It sufficeth that in the performance of your Orisons ye shall not give way unto sleep, and that ye shall fail in nowise in this operation through negligence and voluntarily.

* In the text evidently by a slip the word *grandeur* is repeated *la grandeur la grandeur de Dieu.*

† " *Laissez apart touttes les choses curieuses.*"

74   THE BOOK OF THE SACRED MAGIC

THE ELEVENTH CHAPTER.*

CONCERNING THE SELECTION OF THE PLACE.

E should make the Selection of the Place (for the Operation) before commencing it, and prior to the celebration of the Passover, in order that we may decide upon the same without hindrance, and it is necessary that all things should be prepared.

He who commenceth this Operation in solitude can elect a place according unto his pleasure ; where there is a small wood, in the midst of which you shall make a small Altar, and you shall cover the same with a hut (or shelter) of fine branches, so that the rain may not fall thereon and extinguish the Lamp and the Censer. Around the Altar at the distance of seven paces you shall prepare a hedge of flowers, plants, and green shrubs, so that it may divide the entrance † into two parts ; that is to say, the Interior where the Altar and Tabernacle will be placed after the manner of a Temple ; and the part Exterior, which with the rest of the place will be as a Portico thereunto.

Now if you commence not this Operation in the Country, but perform it in a Town, or in some dwelling-place, I will show unto ye what shall be necessary herein. ‡

Ye shall choose an Apartment which hath a Window, joined unto the which shall be an uncovered Terrace (or

---

* This chapter is previously referred to in the Seventh Chapter in speaking of the Bed-chamber and the Oratory.

† "*L'avenue*"; the modern sense of this word is, of course, a road or path bordered by trees.

‡ Compare the following description with that of Sir Philip Derval's so-called Observatory, in the *Strange Story*, by Bulwer Lytton.

Balcony), and a Lodge (or small room or hut) covered with a roof, but so that there may be on every side windows whence you may be able to see in every direction, and whence you may enter into the Oratory. In the which place * the Evil Spirits shall be able to appear, since they cannot appear within the Oratory itself. In the which place, beside the Oratory towards the quarter of the North, you shall have a roofed or covered Lodge, in the which and from whence one may be able to see the Oratory. I myself also had two large windows made in my Oratory, and at the time of the Convocation of the Spirits, I used to open them and remove both the shutters and the door, so that I could easily see on every side and constrain them † to obey me.

The Oratory should always be clear and clean swept, and the flooring should be of wood, of white pine ; in fine, this place should be so well and carefully prepared, that one may judge it to be a place destined unto prayer.

The Terrace and the contiguous Lodge where we are to invoke the Spirits we should cover with river sand to the depth of two fingers at the least.

The Altar should be erected in the midst of the Oratory ; and if any one maketh his Oratory in desert places, he should build it‡ of stones which have never been worked or hewn, or even touched by the hammer.

The Chamber § should be boarded with pine wood, and a Lamp full of Oil Olive should be suspended therein, the which every time that ye shall have burned your perfume and finished your orison, ye shall extinguish. A handsome Censer of bronze, or of silver if one hath the means, must be placed upon the Altar, the which should in no wise be removed from its place until the Operation

---

* *I.e.*, the Terrace or Balcony.   † *I.e.*, the Spirits.
‡ *I.e.*, the Altar.
§ He here evidently means the Oratory, and not the Bed-chamber described in Chapter VII.

be finished, if one performeth it in a dwelling-house ; for in the open country one cannot do this. Thus in this point as in all the others, we should rule and govern ourselves according unto the means at our disposal.

The Altar, which should be made of wood, ought to be hollow within after the manner of a cupboard, wherein you shall keep all the necessary things, such as the two Robes, the Crown or Mitre, the Wand, the Holy Oils, the Girdle or Belt, the Perfume ; and any other things which may be necessary.

*The second habiliments will be a Shirt or Tunic of linen, large and white, with well and properly made sleeves. The other Robe will be of Crimson or Scarlet Silk with Gold, and it should not be longer than just unto the knees, with sleeves of similar stuff. As for these vestments, there is no particular rule for them ; nor any especial instructions to be followed ; but the more resplendent, clean, and brilliant they are the better will it be. You shall also make a Girdle of Silk of the same colour as the Tunic, wherewithal you shall be girded. You shall have upon your head a beautiful Crown or woven Fillet of Silk and Gold. You shall prepare the Sacred Oil in this manner : Take of myrrh† in tears, one part ; of fine cinnamon, two parts ; of galangal‡ half a part ; and the half of the total weight of these drugs of the best oil olive. The which aromatics you shall mix together according unto the Art of the Apothecary, and shall make thereof a Balsam, the which you shall keep in a glass vial which you shall put within the cupboard (formed by the interior) of the Altar. The Perfume

---

* The Rosicrucian Initiate will note the description of these vestments.

† " *Mirrhe en larmes* ".

‡ ? Galanca, or galanga, an Indian root, used for medicinal purposes. See description of Holy Anointing Oil and Perfume in Exodus xxx.

shall be made thus : Take of Incense in tears * one part ;
of Stacté † half a part ; of Lign Aloes a quarter of a
part ; and not being able to get this wood you shall take
that of cedar, or of rose, or of citron, or any other
odoriferous wood. You shall reduce all these ingredients
into a very fine powder, mix them well together and
keep the same in a box or other convenient vessel. As
you will consume a great deal of this perfume, it will be
advisable to mix enough on the eve of the Sabbath to
last the whole week.

You shall also have a Wand of Almond-tree wood,
smooth and straight, of the length of about from half an
ell to six feet.‡ And ye shall keep the aforesaid things
in good order in the cupboard§ of the Altar, ready for
use in the proper time and place.

Here followeth the manner of ordering oneself and
of operating.

THE TWELFTH CHAPTER.

HOW ONE SHOULD KEEP ONESELF IN ORDER TO CARRY OUT THIS OPERATION WELL.

HIS Operation being truly Divine, it is
necessary once more to treat of and distinguish the present Consecration into
different periods of time.

You shall then understand that during
the two first and two second Moons, no other Consecration must be performed, than that of which we have
already spoken in the Seventh and Eighth foregoing

---

* Olibanum.   † Or storax.

‡ A " brasse " is a fathom ; but here perhaps implies rather an
arm's length : " *Lune brasse enveron ou demi aulne* ".

§ *I.e.*, in the hollow interior of the Altar.

78   THE BOOK OF THE SACRED MAGIC

Chapters,* unto the which I refer you, so as not to be
too prolix.   And I only say unto you, that during the
course of the two first and two second Moons, every
Saturday when ye perform the Orison, ye shall also burn
the Perfume as well in the morning as in the evening ;
and in the two third and last Moons ye shall make the
Prayer and the Perfume thrice daily.

Now here hath the last part of the time arrived ;
here therefore open ye your eyes and be attentive, and
govern yourselves in everything and every place in the
way which I have written unto you.   Have confidence
in God, because if even until then ye have faithfully
observed mine instructions which I have given unto you,
and if your Orisons shall have been made with a righteous
heart and with devotion, there is no manner of doubt that
all things will appear easy unto you, and your own spirit
and your understanding will teach you the manner in
which you should conduct yourself in all points ; because
your Guardian Angel is already about you, though Invisible, and conducteth and governeth your heart, so that
you shall not err.   The two Moons being finished, in
the morning ye shall commence all that is commanded in
the Ninth Chapter,† and further observe this present
Chapter.

When first ye shall enter into the Oratory, leave
your shoes without,‡ and having opened the window,§
ye shall place the lighted coals in the Censer which‖ you
shall have brought with you, you shall light the Lamp,
and take from the Cupboard of the Altar your two Vest-

---

* Which give the instructions for these periods.

† Concerning the two last Moons.

‡ "Put off thy shoes from off thy feet, for the place whereon thou
standest is holy ground."

§ It will be remarked how this point is insisted on.

‖ "Which," apparently, should refer to the coals, and not to
the censer.

ments, the Crown, the Girdle and the Wand, placing them upon the Altar. Then take the Sacred Oil in your left hand, cast some of the Perfume upon the Fire, and place yourself upon your knees,* praying unto the Lord with fervour.

THE ORISON.

" O LORD GOD of Mercy ; God, Patient, Most Benign and Liberal ; Who grantest Thy Grace in a thousand ways, and unto a thousand generations ; Who forgettest the iniquities, the sins, and the transgressions of men ; in Whose Presence none is found innocent ; Who visitest the transgressions of the father upon the children and nephews unto the third and fourth generation ; I know my wretchedness, and that I am not worthy to appear before Thy Divine Majesty, nor even to implore and beseech Thy Goodness and Mercy for the least Grace. But, O Lord of Lords, the Source of Thy Bounty is so great, that of Itself It calleth those who are ashamed by reason of their sins and dare not approach, and inviteth them to drink of Thy Grace. Wherefore, O Lord my God, have pity upon me, and take away from me all iniquity and malice ; cleanse my soul from all the uncleanness of sin ; renew within me my Spirit, and comfort it, so that it may become strong and able to comprehend the Mystery of Thy Grace, and the Treasures of Thy Divine Wisdom. Sanctify me also with the Oil of Thy Sanctification, wherewith Thou hast sanctified all Thy Prophets ; and purify in me therewith all that appertaineth unto me, so that I may become worthy of the Conversation of Thy Holy Angels and of Thy Divine Wisdom, and grant unto me the Power which Thou

* Preferably I should advise upon the Western side of the Altar, and facing therefore the East ; also I would have the cupboard opening upon the Western side, for certain mystical reasons.

hast given unto Thy Prophets over all the Evil Spirits. Amen. Amen."

This is the Prayer which I myself made use of in my Consecration ; the which I give not here to confine you (to a certain form), nor to oblige you to employ the same, nor to tell it you over as I would to a parrot whom I should wish to teach to talk ; but only and solely to give unto you an idea of the manner in which we should pray.

Having finished your Orison, rise from your knees, and anoint the centre* of your forehead with a little of the Sacred Oil ; after this dip your finger into the same Oil, and anoint therewith the four upper corners of the Altar. Touch also with this Holy Oil the Vestments, the Girdle, the Crown, and the Wand, on both sides. You shall also touch the Doors and the Windows of the Oratory. Then with your finger dipped in the Oil you shall write upon the four sides of the Altar these words, so that they may be perfectly clearly written on each side :—

"In whatever place it may be wherein Commemoration of My Name shall be made, I will come unto you and I will bless you."

This being done the Consecration is finished, and then ye shall put the White Tunic and all the other things into the Cupboard of the Altar. Then kneel down and make your ordinary prayer, as is laid down in the Third Chapter ;† and be well ware to take no consecrated thing out of the Oratory ; and during the whole of the ensuing period ye shall enter the Oratory and celebrate the Office with naked feet.

---

* The place of the third eye in the Indian figures of Gods.

† This is apparently a slip for "the Seventh Chapter"; as the Third Chapter is only a short one regarding those who are fitted to undertake the Operation.

THE THIRTEENTH CHAPTER.

CONCERNING THE CONVOCATION OF THE GOOD SPIRITS.

E are now arrived at a point at which ye shall be able to see clearly, having duly followed out and observed the instructions which I have given unto you, and having during all this time served God your Creator with a perfect heart. We are now arrived at the term, wherefore the following morning rise betimes, neither wash yourselves at all nor dress yourselves at all in your ordinary clothes ; but take a Robe of Mourning ; enter the Oratory with bare feet ; go unto the side of the Censer, take the ashes therefrom and place them upon your head ; light the Lamp ; and put the hot coals into the Censer ; and having opened the windows, return unto the door. There prostrate yourself with your face against the ground, and order the Child* to put the Perfume upon the Censer, after which he is to place himself upon his knees before the Altar ; following in all things and throughout the instructions which I have given unto you in the last chapter of the First Book, to which I am here referring.† Humiliate yourself before God and His Celestial Court, and commence your Prayer with fervour, for then it is that you will begin to enflame yourself in praying, and you will see appear an extraordinary and supernatural Splendour which will fill the whole apartment, and will surround you with an inexpressible odour, and this alone will console you and comfort your heart so that you shall call for ever happy the Day of the Lord. Also

---

* See Book I., Chapter XII.

† Because previously when he has mentioned a foregoing chapter, it has been one of those in this Second Book to which he has referred.

the Child* will experience an admirable feeling of con-
tentment in the presence of the Angel. And you shall
continue always your Prayer redoubling your ardour and
fervour, and shall pray the Holy Angel that he may deign
to Sign, and write upon a small square plate of silver
(which you shall have had made for this purpose and
which you shall have placed upon the Altar) another
Sign if you shall have need of it in order to see him ; and
everything which you are to do. As soon as the Angel
shall have made the Sign by writing, and that he shall
have written down some other counsel which may be
necessary unto you, he will disappear, but the splendour
will remain. The which the Child having observed, and
made the sign thereof unto you, you shall command him
to bring you quickly the little plate of silver, and that
which you find written thereon you shall at once copy,
and order the Child to replace it upon the Altar. Then
you shall go forth from the Oratory and leave the
Window open, and the Lamp alight, and during this
whole day you shall not enter into the Oratory ; but shall
make preparation for the day following ; and during the
day you shall speak to none, nor make answer, even were
it your own wife or children or servants ; except to the
Child whom you can send away. Also you shall beforehand have set your affairs in order, and so arranged them
that no embarrassment may be caused you thereby, which
might distract your attention. In the evening when the
Sun shall be set, you shall eat but soberly ; and then you
shall go to rest alone ; and you shall live separated from
your wife during these days.

During Seven Days shall you perform the Ceremonies
without failing therein in any way ; namely, the Day of

---

* If the Operator himself has developed the clairvoyant faculty ;
which the training he has subjected himself to for six months ought to
have greatly aided, and be pure in mind, I can see no necessity for the
employment of a Child as Seer.

the Consecration, the Three Days of the Convocation of the Good and Holy Spirits, and the Three other Days of the Convocation of the Evil Spirits.

Now the second morning after, you are to be prepared to follow the counsel which the Angel will have given you. You will go early unto the Oratory, you will place the lighted charcoal and perfumes in the Censer, you are to relight the Lamp if it be (by that time) extinguished ; and wearing the same Robe of Mourning as of the day before, prostrate with your face towards the ground, you shall humbly pray unto and supplicate the Lord that He may have pity on you, and that He may deign to fulfil your prayer ; that He will grant unto you the vision of His Holy Angels, and that the Elect Spirits may deign to grant unto you their familiar converse. And thus shall ye pray unto the utmost degree that shall be possible unto you, and with the greatest fervour that you can bring into action from your heart, and this during the space of two or three hours. Then quit the Oratory, returning thither at midday for another hour, and equally again in the evening ; then you shall eat after the manner aforesaid, and go to rest. Understand also that the odour and the splendour will in nowise quit the Oratory.

The third day being now arrived, you shall act thus. The evening (before) you shall wash your whole body thoroughly ; and in the morning, being dressed in your ordinary garments, you shall enter into the Oratory, but with naked feet. Having placed the Fire and the Perfumes in the Censer, and lighted the Lamp, you shall put on the White Vestment, and place yourself on your knees before the Altar, to render thanks to God for all His benefits, and firstly for having granted unto you a Treasure so great and so precious. You shall render thanks also unto the Holy Guardian Angels, praying unto them that henceforward they will have you in their care for the whole period of your life ; also that he* will never abandon you, that he will lead you in the Way of the Lord, and that he will watch carefully over you to assist you, and consent unto the present Operation of the Sacred Magic, so that you shall have such Force and Virtue that you may be able to constrain the Spirits accursed of God, unto the Honour of your Creator, and for your own good and that of your neighbour.

And then shall you first be able to put to the test whether you shall have well employed the period of your Six Moons, and how well and worthily you shall have laboured in the quest of the Wisdom of the Lord ; since you shall see your Guardian Angel appear unto you in un-equalled beauty ; who also will converse with you, and speak in words so full of affection and of goodness, and with such sweetness, that no human tongue could express the same. He will animate you unto your great content in the fear of God, making you a recital of the blessings which you have received from God ; and bringing unto your re-membrance the sins by which you have offended Him during the whole period of your life, will instruct you and give unto you the manner in which you shall be able to appease Him by a pure, devout, and regulated life, and by honest and meritorious actions, and such things as God shall ordain unto you. After this he will show unto you the True Wisdom and Holy Magic, and also wherein you have erred in your Operation, and how thenceforward you should proceed in order to overcome the Evil Spirits, and finally arrive at your desired ends. He will promise never to abandon you, but to defend and assist you during the whole period of your life ; on con-dition that you shall obey his commands, and that you shall not voluntarily offend your Creator. In one word, you shall be received by him with such affection that

---

* *I.e.*, your special and particular Guardian Angel.

this description which I here give unto you shall appear a mere nothing in comparison.

Now at this point I commence to restrict myself in my writing, seeing that by the Grace of the Lord I have submitted and consigned you unto a MASTER so great that he will never let you err.

Observe that on the third day you should remain in familiar conversation* with your Guardian Angel. You should quit the Oratory for a short time in the afternoon, remaining without about an hour ; then for the rest of the day you shall remain therein, receiving from the Holy Angel distinct and ample information regarding the Evil Spirits and the manner of bringing them into submission, carefully writing down and taking notes of all these matters. Now, the Sun being set, you shall perform the Evening Orison with the ordinary Perfume, giving thanks unto God in particular for the very great Grace that He hath granted unto you in that day, there also supplicating Him to be propitious unto you and to aid you during your whole life, so that you shall never be able to offend Him. You shall also render thanks unto your Guardian Angel and beseech him not to abandon you.

The Prayer being finished you will see that the Splendour will disappear. Then shall you quit the Oratory, closing the door, but leaving the windows open and the Lamp alight. You shall return as on the preceding days unto your apartment where you shall modestly recreate yourself, and eat your necessary food, then you shall go to rest until the following morning.

* "*En la familiarité et conversation delange.*"

THE FOURTEENTH CHAPTER.

CONCERNING THE CONVOCATION OF THE SPIRITS.*

THOUGH the following advice may be scarcely necessary for the most part, since I have already explained unto you all things necessary to be done ; and also seeing that your Guardian Angel will have sufficiently instructed you in all that you should do ; yet nevertheless I will here declare plainly certain matters unto you, with the idea rather of making the account of the Operation complete in this Book,† and also to give you every opportunity of possessing the matter thoroughly through reading these things many times ; so that having received the Vision of the Angel, you may find yourself thoroughly instructed in all the essential points.

Having then reposed yourself during the night, you shall rise in the morning before dawn, and shall enter into the Oratory ; and having placed the lighted Charcoal in the Censer, light the Lamp also. You shall then robe yourself, taking first the White Vestment, and over this you shall put on that ‡ of Silk and Gold, then the Girdle, and upon your head you shall place the Crown, and you shall lay the Wand upon the Altar. Then, having put the Perfume in the Censer you shall fall upon your knees, and pray unto Almighty God to grant you the Grace to finish your Operation unto the Praise and Glory of His Holy Name, and for your own use and that of your neighbour. Also you shall supplicate your Guardian

---

* *I.e.*, those of a material force ; many being evil, some few inclined to good, most of a mixed nature somewhat good yet the evil predominating in their dispositions.

† *I.e.*, this Second Book of the three constituting the treatise.

‡ *I.e.*, the Red Robe, or Mantle.

OF ABRA-MELIN THE MAGE.   87

Angel to aid you, and to govern your heart with his counsel, and all your senses. After this you shall take the Wand in your right hand, and pray unto God to give unto this Wand as much virtue, force, and power as He gave unto those of MOSES, of AARON, of ELIJAH, and of the other Prophets whose number is infinite.

Now place yourself beside the Altar looking towards the Door and the open Terrace ; or if you be in the Country place yourself at the Western * side, and commence by summoning the Chief Spirits and Princes.

But your Angel will already have instructed you how to convoke them, and will have sufficiently impressed it on your heart.

And as well in this as in the Orison, we should never proceed and act by the mouth only or by written Conjurations alone ; but with a free heart and intrepid courage ; because it is certain that there is more difficulty in convoking the Evil Spirits † than the Good, which latter usually appear more readily when they are first called if it be by persons of good intent ; while the Evil Spirits flee as much as possible all occasion of submitting themselves to man. This is wherefore he who wisheth to constrain them should be upon his guard, and follow out faithfully from point to point the instructions which his Guardian Angel will have given him, and that he im-

---

* " *Ou si vous estez en Campagne mettes vous ducosté du ponant.*" This word "*ponant*" is almost obsolete in modern French, being only employed in a nautical sense, and even then but rarely. It implies the " West," or rather the part of the " Ocean towards the West ". Even in the middle ages this expression was not in wide use. The Occult student will remark here the idea of " turning to the East to pray, and to the West to invoke ". But usually in Magic it is advisable to turn towards the quarter sympathetic in nature with that of the Spirit you wish to summon.

† That is if you convoke them to *serve you.* But all mediæval tradition implies that they are ready enough to come if you are an evil-minded person wishing to make a pact with them to obtain magical force, *i.e.* a Göetic Magician as opposed to an Initiate Adept.

88   THE BOOK OF THE SACRED MAGIC

presseth them well upon his memory following them from
point to point ; seeing that while no Spirit Good or Evil
can know the secrets of your heart before you yourself
bring the same to light, unless God Who alone knoweth all
things should manifest them ; they (the Spirits) nevertheless can penetrate into and understand that which you are
thinking by means of your actions and your words.*
This is the reason why he who wisheth properly to convoke and conjure the Spirits, should first well consider
the following Conjuration ; and afterward perform it
with feeling and freely by heart ; and not by writing,
because in using that composed by others, the Spirits
thence judge that we ourselves are ignorant, and render
themselves straightway more intractable and stubborn.†
The Evil Spirits be about you, though invisible, and they
keenly examine whether he who conjureth them is
courageous or timid, whether he is prudent, and whether
he hath a true faith in God Who can perform all things
with ease. We can constrain them (the Spirits), and
force them to appear ; but a few words ill pronounced by
an ill-intentioned person only produce an effect against
the person himself who ignorantly pronounceth them ;
and an individual of such a character should in no way
undertake this Operation, for such would be the true way
to make a mock of God and to tempt Him.

    * This is why in religious and magical writings such stress is
laid on the importance of controlling the *thoughts ;* which are as it
were our prototypical speech and action in all matters of importance.
Modern thought-reading would alone suggest this to persons unskilled
in Occultism.
    † " *Les Esprits jugent parla denostre ignoranse et serendent plus
reveches et ostinez.*" The Initiate knows the value of an Invocation
written by himself, in harmony with and expressing exactly his will
and idea. But this does not deny the utility of many of the Conjurations handed down by tradition.

OF THE CONJURATIONS.

I have many times repeated unto you that the Fear of God is the principal subject of the instruction of your Guardian Angel, against which you should never commit any fault, even if it be but slight.

Firstly : You should perform the Conjuration in your mother tongue,* or in a language that you well understand, and conjure the Spirits by the authority of and their obedience to the Holy Patriarchs, rehearsing unto them examples of their ruin and fall, of the sentence which God hath pronounced against them, and of their obligation unto servitude ; and how on one side and on another they have been vanquished by the Good Angels and by Wise Men ; all which points you will have had plenty of opportunity to study in the Sacred Writings during the Six Moons (of preparation). Also you shall menace them, in case they are unwilling to obey, with calling unto your aid the Power of the Holy Angels over them. Your Guardian Angel will also have instructed you to perform this Convocation with modesty, and in no wise to be timid, but courageous, yet in moderation, however, without too overbearing hardiness and bravery. And in case of their being inclined to resist, and unwilling to obey you, you must not on that account give way to anger, because thus you will only do injury to yourself ; and they will ask nothing better, it being exactly what they would be endeavouring to do ; but (on the contrary) with an intrepid heart, and putting your whole trust in God, with a tranquil heart you shall exhort them to yield, letting them see that you have put all your confidence in the Living and Only God, reminding them how

---

* Yet the advantage of its being in a language which you do not immediately associate with the things of every-day life is great, *provided always that you understand the words and repeat them and pronounce them correctly.*

powerful and potent He is ; thus, therefore, govern yourself, using prudence towards them.

And communicate unto them also the Form* in
the which you wish them to appear ; the which you can
not determine, nor even themselves, but you ought the
evening before to have demanded this from your Guardian Angel, who knoweth better than you your nature
and constitution, and who understandeth the forms which
can terrify you, and those of which you can support the
sight.†

And you must not think that this can be done otherwise, as certain Accursed Persons write; that is to say,
by means of Seals, and Conjurations, and Superstitious
Figures, and Pentacles, and other Abominations, written
by Diabolical Enchanters ;‡ for this would be the coin
wherewith the Hideous SATAN would buy you for his
slave.

But let your whole trust be in the Arm, the Power,
and the Force of God Almighty ; then shall you be in
all safety, and the Guard of your Angel will defend you
from all dangers. This is why you should have good
courage, and have confidence that no adversity can happen
unto you. Observing then the doctrine that your Angel
will have given unto you, and persevering in placing all
your trust in God, at length they will appear in the form
commanded upon the Terrace, upon the sand ; when,
according to the advice and doctrine received from your

* This recalls the phrase so frequent in Conjurations, in which
the Spirits are commanded to appear "in human form without any
deformity or tortuosity".

† Because some of the Demonic forms are so terrible that the
shock of their sight might cause a person of a nervous temperament
to lose his reason.

‡ I must again repeat that it is only evil and perverted symbols
which come under this denunciation of Abraham the Jew ; for nearly
all Pentacles and Seals are the Symbols and Sigils of Divine and
Angelic Names.

Holy Angel, and as I will clearly teach you in the following Chapter, you shall propound your demand, and
you shall receive from them their oath.*

The Spirits which we should convoke on the first day
are the Four Superior Princes,† whose Names will be
written in the Nineteenth Chapter, and this is the Conjuration of the First Day.

THE CONJURATION OF THE SECOND DAY.

On the following day, having performed the ordinary Orison, and the aforesaid Ceremonies, you shall briefly
repeat the aforesaid Conjuration unto the said Spirits,
bringing to their remembrance their promises and Oaths
made on the preceding day to send unto you the Eight
Sub-Princes ;‡ and address the Conjuration unto all the
Twelve together, and in a little while they will appear
visibly, the Eight Sub-Princes in the form which hath
been commanded them ; and they will promise and swear
unto you (allegiance), as will be more fully shown in the
following Chapter.

The Names of the Eight Sub-Princes are described
hereafter in the Nineteenth § Chapter.

THE CONJURATION OF THE THIRD DAY.

The Conjuration of the Third Day is the same as
that of the Second Day, seeing that we are then to remind the Eight Sub-Princes of their Promises and Oaths
(of Allegiance) ; and we are to call and convoke them
with all their adherents, and then they do appear once

---

* *I.e.*, of allegiance to you.

† The four Superior Spirits and Princes are : Lucifer, Leviathan,
Satan, and Belial.

‡ The Eight Sub-Princes are : Astaroth, Magoth, Asmodeus,
Beelzebuth ; Oriens, Païmon, Ariton, and Amaymon.

§ By a very evident slip, " *Chapitre* IX." is written in the MS.
instead of XIX.

more in visible forms, the whole particular cohorts of each will appear also invisibly, surrounding the Eight Sub-Princes. But while invoking God your Lord for strength and surety, and your Holy Angel for counsel and assistance, never forget what the latter will have taught you, for it is a necessary point.

Here followeth the Fifteenth Chapter which teacheth what we should demand from the Spirits, who are divided into three classes.

THE FIFTEENTH CHAPTER.

CONCERNING WHAT YOU SHOULD DEMAND OF THE SPIRITS WHO ARE DIVIDED INTO THREE DIFFERENT TROOPS AND CONVOKED ON THREE SEPARATE DAYS.

THE Demands we should make to the Spirits are of three different kinds.

THE FIRST DEMAND.

The Demand of the First Day when the Four Superior Princes shall have visibly appeared, you shall make according unto the Order of the Angel :—

Firstly : The Proposition by what Virtue, Power and Authority you make your demands unto them ; that is to say by the Virtue of God our Lord Who hath made them subject unto all His creatures, and brought them to your feet.*

Secondly : † That your object is not at all a malign curiosity, but (one tending) unto the Honour and Glory

---

* " *Qui les asoumis atouttes ses Creatures et avos pieds.*"

† This whole paragraph is difficult of clear translation by literal rendering, so I give the MS. text : " *Secondement que vostre fin nest point curiosité maligne mais alhonneur et gloire de Dieu et alutilité propre et acelle de tout le genre humain etpourtant toutte ces fois que*

OF ABRA-MELIN THE MAGE. 93

of God, and to your own good and that of all the Human Race. That further, every time that you shall summon them, by whatever Sign or Word, and in whatever Time and Place, and for whatever occasion and service, they shall have to appear immediately without any delay, and obey your commands. And that in case they shall have some legitimate hindrance hereto, they are to send unto you some other Spirits assigning then and there such as shall be capable and potent to accomplish and obey your will and your demand in their place. And that they shall promise and swear to observe this by the most rigorous Judgment of God, and by the most severe punishment and chastisement of the Holy Angels, inflicted upon them. And that they will consent to obey, and that the Four Sovereign Princes will name unto you the Eight Sub-Princes, whom they will send in their place to take the Oath as I have already said, to appear at once on the following morning when commanded by you ; and that they will duly send the Eight Sub-Princes.

For greater certainty, quit the Altar now, and go towards the Door which openeth on to the Terrace, advancing your right hand beyond.* Make each one of them touch the Wand, and take the Oath upon that Wand.

vous les appellerez avec quelquesoit signe ou parole etenquelquesoit temps et Lieu etpourquelle soit occasion etservile dabort sans aucunement retarder ayent aparoitre etobeissent avos commandemens etaucas quils eussent un empechemen Legitime quils ayent avous envoyer dautres esprits enles nommant presentement ceux quiseront capable etpuissan pourobeir etaccomplir vostre volonte et vostre demande en leur place etquils vous promeltent et jurent dobserver cela par le tresrigoureux jugement de Dieu etpar latres grande peine et chatiment dessts anges sur eux ils consentiront dobeir et Les 4 princes souverains vous nommeront les 8 sousprinces quils vous enveront enleurplase aleurfaire preter le serment comme jelay deja dit deparoitre dabort," etc. The writer of this manuscript never uses the slightest punctuation, and paragraphs are infrequent.

* *I.e.*, beyond the Door, but being careful not to go out on to the Terrace yourself.

THE DEMAND OF THE SECOND DAY.

THE Eight Sub-Princes being invoked, you shall make unto them the same demand and the same admonition which you have (already) made unto the Four Sovereign Princes. And further you shall request from these four, that is to say, from ORIENS, PAIMON, ARITON, and AMAIMON ; that each of them shall assign and consign unto you your Familiar Spirit, which from the day of your birth they are compelled to give unto you. These will be given and furnished unto you with their dependants and will afterwards obey you. It is for you to demand from these the other Spirits which you may wish to have ; but seeing that they be infinite in number, and one more skilful in service than another, one for one matter, another for another ; you shall make a selection of the Spirits whom you wish, and you shall put outside upon the Terrace a written list of their names for the Eight Sub-Princes (to see), and you shall require from these (latter) the Oath, as you did from the Four Superior Princes, that the following morning they shall have to appear before you together with all the Spirits whose names you shall have given in writing, and also your Familiar Spirits.

THE DEMAND OF THE THIRD DAY.

THE Eight Sub-Princes having presented all the Spirits as you have directed them, you shall command that ASTAROT* with all his following shall appear visibly in the Form which the Angel shall have prescribed unto you ; and immediately you shall see a Great Army, and all under the same Form. You shall propound unto them the same demand, which you have already made unto the Princes, and you shall cause them to take Oath

* Written " *Atarot* " by a slip in the MS.

OF ABRA-MELIN THE MAGE. 95

to observe the same ; that is to say, that every time that you shall call one of them by his name, that he shall at once appear in such Form and Place as shall please you, and that he shall punctually execute that which you shall have commanded him. All having sworn, you shall put outside the entry* of the Door, all the Signs of the Third Book which belong unto ASTAROT † *alone*, and make him swear thereon, also ordaining unto them‡ that in cases when it may not seem fit unto you to command them verbally, that as soon as you shall take one of these Signs in your hand and move it from its place that the Spirit marked in the Sign shall do and execute that which the Sign beareth, and that which your intimation § joined thereto shall indicate ; also that in the case that in the Sign ‖ none of them shall be specially named, that all in general shall be obliged promptly and readily to perform the Operation commanded ; and that if also in the time to come, other (Signs or) Symbols be made by you which be not here ¶ included, that then also they (the Spirits under Astarot) shall be equally bound to observe and execute them also. And when the Oath hath been taken, cause the Prince in the Name of the rest to touch the Wand.

After this, remove those Symbols from the Doorway ; and call MAGOT, and after him ASMODEE, and lastly BELZEBUD ; and act with all these as you have done with

* *I.e.*, upon the sand on the Terrace.
† Again erroneously "*Atarot*".
‡ *I.e.*, unto the subservient Spirits of Astaroth.
§ *I.e.*, whether Verbal, or Mental, or by Gesture.
‖ Again note that the whole of the operations of this Magic of Abra-Melin and of Abraham the Jew depends on these Symbols, so that it is not the true and sacred pentacles and symbols which he condemns ; but erroneous and corrupted ones made use of ignorantly.
¶ *I.e.*, in those which the Operator has written down from the Third Book, and placed at the entry of the Door for Astaroth to take oath upon.

ASTAROT ; and all their Symbols having been sworn unto, put them aside in order in a certain place, so arranged that you can easily distinguish one from another, as regards the subject, operation, or effect, for which they have been made, and unto which they belong.

This being done, you shall call ASTAROT and ASMODEE together, with their common Servitors,* and shall propound unto them their Symbols ; and having made them swear in the forementioned manner, you shall call in similar fashion ASMODEE and MAGOT, with their Servitors, and shall make them take oath upon their Signs in the aforesaid manner.

And thus shall you observe this method with the Four other Sub-Princes ; † but first of all convoke them with their common Servitors, and make them swear upon the common Signs, then AMAIMON and ARITON together, and finally each one apart, as in the first case. ‡

And when you have put back all the Symbols into their proper place, request from *each* of these last Four § your Familiar Spirit, and make them repeat its Name, which you shall at once write down, together with the time during which they shall be obliged to serve you. Then you shall propound unto them the Signs of the Fifth Chapter of the Third Book ; ‖ and shall make them not only swear upon these Symbols (collectively), but also each one (separately), that from this time forward he will

---

* *I.e.*, Servitors belonging equally to these two Sub-Princes together.

† *I.e.*, Oriens, Paimon, Ariton, and Amaimon.   Ariton is often called Egin or Egyn in other works on Magic.

‡ *I.e.*, following the order of the classification in the Nineteenth Chapter of this Second Book.

§ *I.e.*, Oriens, Paimon, Ariton, and Amaimon ; one Spirit from each for a Familiar.

‖ Entitled : " How one may retain the Familiar Spirits, bound or free, in whatsoever form ".

OF ABRA-MELIN THE MAGE.   97

observe duly and with diligence the six hours destined ; *
and you shall cause them to promise to serve you with
fidelity, performing all which they are obliged to do, and
that you shall command their (services) ; and that they
shall not in the slightest degree be false and lying as regardeth you ; also, that if by chance you should assign
over one of them unto another person, that he shall act as
faithfully by him as by yourself ; and, lastly, that they are
to fulfil, perform, and execute, that which God for their
Chastisement hath destined unto them for Sentence (of
Judgment).

You shall then observe this form with all the Princes,
and until all the Symbols shall be sworn to, with the
Four Familiar Spirits and the others dominating (them).

THE SIXTEENTH CHAPTER.

CONCERNING THE SENDING THEM AWAY.

CONCERNING the sending away of the
Spirits as well during the Three Days, as
hereafter :—

It is not necessary to observe many
Ceremonies in order to send away the
Spirits,† because they themselves are only too glad to be

---

* *I.e.*, so that each of the four Familiars shall serve a fourth part
of the twenty-four hours of the day, that is six hours.

† However in all Magical Works great stress is laid on the
importance of licensing a Spirit invoked in the Operation to depart,
and if he be unwilling, of even compelling him against his will to
return to his place. It must be remembered here, in this Operation
of Abraham the Jew, that not only his Oratory but his Bed-chamber
also is kept pure and consecrated, and therefore it would be next to
impossible for an Evil Spirit to break through to attack him. But in
all Magical Evocations by the Circle, the Magician should never quit
the same, without having licensed and even forced the Evil Spirits to
depart; as cases are on record of the Operator experiencing sudden

far away from you. This is wherefore you need not otherwise license them to depart ; that is to say that during the
Three Days, having finished speaking with the Four
Sovereign Princes, and afterwards with the Eight Sub-
Princes, and received their Oath (of allegiance), you shall
say unto them that for the present they can go unto their
destined place ; and that every time that they shall be
summoned, let them remember their Oath made upon the
Symbols.

(And you shall send away) the Familiar Spirits and
all other Spirits with the aforesaid words.

It is true, however, that as regardeth the Familiar
Spirits you shall tell them that at the time when they are
on guard-duty they shall remain near you visible or invisible, in whatever form shall please you, in order to
serve you during the destined Six Hours.

THE SEVENTEENTH CHAPTER.

WHAT WE SHOULD ANSWER UNTO THE INTERROGATIONS OF THE SPIRITS, AND HOW WE SHOULD RESIST THEIR DEMANDS.

HE Wicked Devil knoweth full well that
you are in no way obliged unto him, nd
that you have commenced this Operation
under the Grace and Mercy of God, and
under the protection and defence of the
Holy Angels ; nevertheless, he will not fail to try his

death. I myself was present on an occasion when in the Evocation
by the Circle, the Magician incautiously having stooped forward and
outward just over the limit of the Circle, received a shock like that
from a powerful electric battery, which nearly threw him down, struck
the Magical Sword from his hand, and sent him staggering back to
the centre of the Circle. Compare also with this incident Allan Fen-
wick's experience in the *Strange Story*, when his hand accidentally
went beyond the limits of the Circle when he was replenishing the
Lamps during the Evocation.

OF ABRA-MELIN THE MAGE. 99

fortune, and he will seek to turn you aside from the Veritable Path ; but be you constant and courageous, and swerve not in any way, either to the right hand or to the left. If he showeth himself proud with you, render unto him the like, and in your turn show him your pride. If he be humble, be in no wise too rude and severe toward him, but be moderate in all things. If he asketh you some matter, you shall make answer unto him according to the instruction which the Guardian Angel shall have given you ; and understand that the Four Princes,* more than all the rest, will powerfully tempt you, saying unto you : " *Who is he who hath given thee* so great authority ? " They will reproach you with your hardihood and presumption in summoning them, knowing how powerful they are, and contrariwise, how weak and sinful you yourself are. They will reproach you with your sins, and will especially seek to dispute with you concerning your religion and your faith in God : if you be a Jew they will tell you that your faith and your religion have been refuted by God Himself, and that you observe not the True Law as it should be (observed) : also if you be a Pagan they will say, What hath God to do with you or His Creatures either, seeing that you know not God ? if you be a Christian they will say unto you, What business is it of yours to have to do with Hebrew Ceremonies which are tainted with idolatry, and the like ? But let none of this disquiet you in the least ; answer them in few words, and laughingly, that it is none of their business to discuss these matters with you, and to deliver their opinions concerning them ; and that although you may be a worthless wretch and a great sinner, you will yet hope that the True and Only God, Who hath created the Heaven and the Earth, and Who hath condemned them† and brought them into submission under

* *Viz. :* Lucifer, Leviathan, Satan, and Belial.
† *I.e.*, the Demons and Evil Spirits generally.

your feet, will forgive you your sins, both now and in future, whatever may be the religion which you profess. (Further that) you wish to know, understand, confess, and honour no other than the Great and Only God, the Lord of Light, by Whose Power, Virtue, and Authority you command them to obey you.

When you shall have spoken unto them thus, then will they sing another song, telling you that if you wish them to serve and to be obedient unto you, that you must first come to terms with them. Then shall you answer them on this wise :—

" God our Lord hath condemned and sentenced you * to serve me, and I do not treat as an equal with those who are accustomed to obey ".

Then will they demand of you some sacrifice or courtesy if you wish to be served and obeyed promptly. You shall reply that sacrifice is not to be made unto them, but rather unto the only God.

They will then entreat you not to hinder or bring to shame by means of this Wisdom any of their Devotees and Enchanters in their operations and enchantments. You shall then make answer that you are obliged to pursue the Enemies of God and the Lord, and to re-press their malice, and also to save and defend your neighbour, and any who are offended and hurt by them.

Then with much verbiage, and an infinitude of different ways will they make severe attacks upon you, and even the Familiar Spirits will rise up against you in their turn. These latter will demand and beseech of you that you will in no way give them over unto others (to serve them). Hold firm, however, and promise nothing either to one class (of Spirits) or another ; but reply to them that every true and brave man is obliged to aid and serve his friends to the best of his ability, and with all his

* The Demons generally.

possessions, among the which they must assuredly also be comprised.

When at length they see that they have lost all hope of making you prevaricate, and that they can obtain nothing notwithstanding all their requests ; they will definitely surrender, and will ask nothing else of you unless it be that you shall not be too rude and insulting in commanding them. You shall make answer to this, that if they prove themselves to be obedient and prompt in serving you, that it may be that your Angel, by whose instruction and command you are governing yourself, may instruct you not to be so rigid and severe with them if they shall obey, and that in such case you will act as may be right.

THE EIGHTEENTH CHAPTER.

HOW HE WHO OPERATETH SHOULD BEHAVE AS REGARDETH THE SPIRITS.

E have already seen how one should constrain the Spirits, and what one should ask of them ; also how to dismiss them without hurt, and how we should make answer unto their demands and presentments.*

All that I am about to say unto you now is superfluous, because it is certain that any one who shall have observed with a true heart and firm resolution the advice which I have given regarding the Six Moons, will be instructed with so much thoroughness and clearness by his Guardian Angel, that no doubtful point will present itself which he will not be able easily to clear up of himself.

We have also already sufficiently shown how on every or any occasion, he who operateth should comport

* In the original : " *demandes etapparitions* ".

himself as regardeth the Spirits ; that is to say as their Lord, and not as their Servitor. Yet in all matters there should be a reasonable mean, seeing that we are not treating with men, but with Spirits, of whom each one knoweth more than the whole Universe together.

Now if you shall make some demand unto a Spirit, and he shall refuse to execute it ; first well and carefully examine and consider whether it be in the power and nature of the Spirit to whom you make such demand, to fulfil the same. For one Spirit knoweth not all things, and that which appertaineth unto the one, another knoweth not. For this reason, see that ye well take heed before endeavouring to force them to perform a matter. Yet if, however, the Inferior Spirits be disobedient, you shall call their Superiors, and remind them of the oaths which they have taken unto you, and of the chastisement which awaiteth the breaking of such vows.

And immediately, on beholding your steadfastness, they will obey you ; but should they not, you ought then to invoke your Guardian Angel, whose chastisement they will quickly feel.

Yet, notwithstanding, we should never employ harsh means, in order to have that which we can obtain by gentleness and courtesy.*

If during the Invocation they should appear with tumult and insolence, fear nothing ; neither give way to anger ; but appear to make no account thereof. Only show them the Consecrated Wand, and if they continue to make a disturbance, smite upon the Altar twice or thrice therewith, and all will be still.

It should be noted, that after you shall have licensed

---

* Let me here once again insist on the absolute necessity in Occult working of being courteous, *even to the Evil Spirits ;* for the Operator who is insolent and overbearing will speedily lay himself open to obsession by a Spirit of like nature, the which will bring about his ultimate downfall.

OF ABRA-MELIN THE MAGE. 103

them to depart, and they shall have disappeared, you shall take the Censer from the top of the Altar, and having put perfume therein, take it out of the Oratory on to the Terrace whereon the Spirits shall have appeared, and you shall perfume the place all round ; for otherwise the Spirits might work some evil unto persons entering by chance therein.

Now should you be willing to content yourself with the Symbols which be in the Third Book here following ; you shall the day after take away all the Sand from the Terrace and cast it into a secret place ; but above all things take care not to throw it either into a river or into the navigable sea.

But should you desire to procure for yourself various other Symbols and Secrets, leave the Sand and all things in place, as we shall also describe more particularly in the last chapter.

Also, should you wish it, you can retain your arrangements in place, and keep the Apartment of the Oratory proper and clean, as well as the Altar ; which latter you may place in a corner, should it incommode you in the centre of the room. For in this Apartment, if it be not contaminated nor profaned, you may every Saturday enjoy the presence of your Guardian Angel ; the which is one of the most sublime things which you can desire in this Sacred Art.

THE FIRST TWO MONTHS

recisely a quarter of an hour before Sunrise ye shall enter into your Oratory, open the window, and place yourselves upon your knees before the Altar, turning your face towards the window; and devoutly and with boldness ye shall invoke the Name of the Lord, thanking Him for all the grace which He hath given and granted unto you from your infancy until now; then with humility shall ye humble yourselves unto Him, and confess unto Him entirely all your sins; supplicating Him to be willing to pardon you and remit them. Ye shall also supplicate Him that in the time to come He may be willing and pleased to regard you with pity and grant you His grace and goodness to send unto you His Holy Angel, who shall serve unto you as a Guide, and lead you ever in His Holy Way and Will...

When ye shall have performed your orations, close the window, and go forth from the Oratory; so that no one may be able therein to enter; and ye shall not yourselves enter again until the evening when the Sun shall be set. Then shall ye enter therein afresh, and shall perform your prayer in the same manner as in the morning."

From the instructions of the Sacred Magic
(See pages 64-69 of the facsimile.)

20 March, 1973

The only thing that slightly worries me is that all the prayers for the six months are for *my* salvation. I shall, therefore, commence and close each oration with the Lord's prayer.

Tonight it rained. A month or so ago I thought that if it did not rain the night before... (Ah, my first orison will be made in a plastic mac.)

(I was hoping it would rain as I felt the rain would not only clear the atmosphere but also be symbolically cleansing.)

21 March

Have begun Operation. Rose at six, washed thoroughly, put on clean clothes and entered Oratory. Still raining. Prayed again at dusk. Still raining. The dogs began fighting and making a terrible noise just beside the Oratory at one point. I felt a strong malevolent presence trying to interfere, tempting me with lazy peace and power if I should become his friend. He departed after five seconds. I do not know whether this is a good or bad start. I am torn apart and everything is in a sort of senseless limbo – but my head behind all this keeps on smiling.

(Throughout the six months I often experienced what I interpreted as malevolent energies. I did not see or hear them, but felt them.)

22 March

From now onwards I will only note that I have correctly kept to the Operation – which I did today. Found in Exodus 23, xx-xxii:

'Behold, I send an Angel before thee, to keep thee in the way, and to bring thee into the place which I have prepared.

'Beware of him, and obey his voice, provoke him not; for he will not pardon your transgressions: for my name is in him.

'But if thou shalt indeed obey his voice, and do all that I speak; then I will be an enemy unto his enemies, and an adversary unto thy adversaries.'

The atmosphere is very difficult around me. Obstacles are

being thrown up and I am clumsily stumbling down the path. (The dogs had placed a pile of bones including half a sheep's skull and two rams' horns a few feet from the entrance to the Oratory.)

23 March
Leviticus 19, xxxi: 'Regard not them that have familiar spirits, neither seek after wizards, to be defiled by them...' I presume this to be an esoteric law as regards the first phrase. I look forward to reading the *Zohar*. And further, Leviticus 20, xxvii:

'A man also or a woman that hath a familiar spirit, or that is a wizard, shall surely be put to death: they shall stone them with stones: their blood shall be upon them.'

I kept correctly to the Operation. Tonight Frances and I were married by ourselves in the eyes of God. A sudden urge and rush to do this, but something about which we have thought previously. So may the Lord will it.

24 and 25 March
Last night, for the first time, forgot to make an entry. As a form of penance, had freezing wash this morning which in fact I almost enjoyed. The Operation was correctly kept to. Also, I did half-an-hour's healing exercise in the afternoon to fix my weak bladder that has been getting me out of bed once or twice every night. It seems to have worked as I did not have to relieve myself last night. Feel that I am now ready to continue exercises to achieve exteriorization. Am also re-working Mouni Sadhu's book *The Tarot. (For details of all books mentioned in the Diary, see Bibliography.)*

And today the Operation was kept to, with incense. Also half-an-hour's exercise this afternoon.

26 March
Last night I retained a form of consciousness through the early part of my sleep. For a second, it almost frightened me and a voice within me said: 'Well may you be fearful; come join with me.' It was murky and then blissful, at points bathing in a calm ecstasy. Operation kept to. As I prayed this evening, something brushed over my head. I do not know what it was or whether it frightened me. And I wonder now about sleeping – with a smile. The atmosphere is strained.

27 March
Operation kept to. Life more tranquil.

28 March
Operation kept to. Forty-five minutes' exercise this afternoon. Every night, though, since I started, my head spins and rushes, elated then deflated, energy rushing through me. I like: II Samuel 7, xx-xxix.

29 March
Operation kept to. Thirty minutes' exercise this afternoon. I seem to have lost my sense of time in terms of days. Am in a peculiarly stressed condition with periodic feelings that I am about to crack up. I am also fighting another battle with those around me. My prayers are becoming more intense and today I felt something, something infinitely powerful and Good that terrified me. Still with my smile, nothing will stop me, but it is heavier than anything I have ever conceived of in the whole of my life (or even approached experiencing) – and how much deeper will it get? The answer, of course, is obvious. That written on 7 February *(in my diary)* seems very real. Ah, but always my smile... perhaps if I did not ever leave the Oratory...I have a slight vision of His mercy and bliss.

This is what I wrote on 7 February:

I have just read a passage in Israel Regardie's *The Tree of Life* on the sacred Operation of Abra-Melin which is relevant as I begin preparing:

'By this time (4th/5th month) he will have entered that state of Dryness of which Mystics of all time have spoken, that horrid psychological state in which all the powers of the soul seem dead and the mind's vision closes in dumb protest, as it were, against the harsh discipline of the oath. A thousand and one seductions will tend to lure the Operator from the contemplation of the end he has chosen, and a thousand and one ways of breaking the oath in spirit...And it will appear that the mind itself will run wild, warning the theurgist *(magician)* to quit... Constantly will it seek to frighten him with inordinate fears relating to health of body and mind. Against all these madnesses – fatal if he so much as succumbs to one temptation – there is only one remedy: the discipline of the oath taken at the beginning; to continue in the labour of invoking for six months the Holy Guardian Angel... It may be that with the third and last period this "Dark Night of the Soul" will pass slowly and imperceptibly, and then will arise the soft rose and pink grandeur of the Dawn, to be followed by the bright daylight of the Knowledge and Conversation, with the Beatific vision and the Perfume so sweet and sustaining to sense and soul, of the Holy Guardian Angel.'

Well, forewarned is forearmed. Ah, but if it is all done in total love and desire...If the discipline is seen only as the cogs to start the motor...We shall see.

30 March
Operation kept to. After this evening's prayer, I feel stronger and comforted, and it is the first night since beginning that I feel calm. I see a vision. (Heavily bracketed: I spent £19, almost our last money, on toys – chemistry-set and meccano – to keep my head together if it feels like splitting in the future.)

31 March
Operation kept to. Personal discipline slack.

1 April
Operation kept to. Any description of the emotions and energies involved would be futile – the terms of reference do not exist, except for another man who has performed it, or similar. *(This was the beginning of the inner experience of intense duality, exacerbated by a very real sense of a new electric energy field or force passing through my brain and my whole body.)*

2 April
Operation kept to. Personal discipline still slack.

3 April
Operation kept to. Personal discipline still slack. I shall change it when I start writing again – but should it be strict now or is that asking too much considering the other strains? Is that a joke?

4 and 5 April
And I forgot to make an entry last night: Operation kept to with some sort of clear light in vision. Those strange mystic and fearful feelings in His Grace that would mean nothing on paper, that if

written would almost be a betrayal. And the formula INRI brings me comfort.

(INRI, according to esoteric tradition, can not only be trans-lated as 'Jesus of Nazareth King of the Jews', but also as 'In us reigns Christ' or 'All nature is regenerated by fire.')

Jeremiah 20, x (he is being mocked for prophesying): '... All my familiars watched for my halting, saying, Peradventure he will be enticed, and we shall prevail against him, and we shall take our revenge on him.' Here is admitted, for the first time, that a prophet of God has familiars – unlike [see entry of 23 March].

Operation kept to. Everything tranquil until the *I Ching* advised to beware of the balance overtoppling. So I hold to myself and attempt to persevere correctly but with difficulty. *(Throughout the Operation I consulted the Chinese oracle, the* I Ching. *This book is an ancient and very insightful treatise which one consults either through throwing coins or picking stalks in a certain sequence. The advice it gives is very metaphysical and often enigmatic and can, therefore, be inter-preted at several levels. At the time I related to the* I Ching *as if it were a close and trusted friend.)*

6 April

Operation kept to. This evening in my oration a moment of great wonder as my Master's presence was known, a conversation almost. This cannot be written about, but my heart is known. *(My belief system included, and still includes, the idea that there exist perfected human beings, enlightened beings, Masters of Compassion - women and men who have completed their learning cycle of education through human incarnation, who now exist in the invisible inner dimensions and whenever possible aid the spiritual growth of humanity. The existence of these perfected teachers is taught, without exception, in all esoteric traditions. I assumed that I was being aided and intuitively guided by one of these Beings. I did not at that particular time know which of these Teachers was guiding me.)*

Later, again, I threw the *I Ching* (to confirm?) and received the sublime Hexagram 2 'The Sublime.' So strange and amazing to remember now the last time that I threw it for such an important time, on my birthday for a message/advice on the coming year, and received Hexagram 1 'The Creative,' equally sublime.

If ever those following the Path should doubt the universality *(of the spiritual path)*, perhaps my Christianity aided by this most magic of books might help. *(I was touched at the time by the fact that while I related to myself as being Christian, I could also draw on the*

wisdom of an Eastern Confucian book of wisdom. I was also touched by
the fact that I was a magician – often thought of as heretical – yet
completely trusting in Christ. My approach to Christianity, of course,
was distinctly outside the formal churches and is what is often called
Gnostic or Rosicrucian.) Ah, the bliss and importance of today. How
can I offer sufficient thanks? With that smile?

7 April
Operation kept to.

8 April
Operation kept to.

9 April
This morning a time of crisis, a time that held fear and the promise
of total change. It is extremely heavy and I am almost frightened.
The vision moves between personal sublimity and a split vulner-
ability. The top of my head feels as though it will split open and I
am drained of strength. Perhaps this is the beginning of that time
when the unconscious flows freely and all must be encountered.
I am wasted and would almost spend all my time in the Oratory.
Maybe I am moving too fast and intensely and must calm somewhat and wait for the last two months... But I should be (and am)
joyful that anything is happening. I have no terms of reference for
how I should control my behaviour, even if it should be controlled.
I yearn for total peace or total distraction – anything else is painful.
But I keep on smiling. And I have such strange thoughts about my
past and future. How much of this is evasive fantasy, how much
real? Yes, my soul, things are moving. The fight has begun and I
must take up the sword to do battle – or am I, the battlefield,
innocent? My state of mind is apparent. But still, lurking behind,
my smile in the knowledge of the fantasy of this dung-heap and
His infinite Grace, Love and Mercy – and Judgement.
     Half-an-hour's exercise this afternoon. Exteriorization control-
led, closer.
     Operation kept to.

10 and 11 April
Forgot to make entry last night (excuse: arrival of a guest). Operation kept to. It is becoming increasingly intense and great changes
are occurring. I have encountered some...? nasties and am being

taught how to behave and treat them. I don't know how heavy
they are and what is to come. But when I feel strong, I recognize
Lucifer himself and his area of power as nothing beside the song
of the harmony of the heavens. And every cloud is just a speck of
dust thrown up by His footprints – as the waters cover the sea. And
I feel my Master's protective yet righteous presence over me. It is
all too bizarre and awful.

Operation kept to. Slightly less intense due to presence of
guest. I must readjust. There is a conflict here in that my weakness
makes behaving lovingly and yet holding truly to discipline (in
emotion) difficult. But I feel my Master as I pray.

12 April

Prayers said. More people have arrived, uninvited and unexpect-
edly, to test the situation. I have broken off from reading the Bible
to write this. Will I do the two hour's study? (No – one hour and
a quarter or less.)

13 April

Operation kept to.

14 April

Operation kept to. A difficult time within me. Our guest now
believes in Him and His Glory. Glory to Him. And what miserable
worm am I? Worthiness – this terrible question of worthiness. And
everything is vanity and I am wandering in a grey murkiness of
my own making when I am not at prayer. Worthiness, worthiness?
The smile is no longer needed – only a shame in my hypocrisy. My
hypocrisy.

(I remember the incident with the guest really well. We were
outside in the landscape and suddenly we went into one of those
silences in which everything is sensed and electric. I suggested
that she look at the sky and as her focus expanded upwards and
outwards she entered into an altered state of mystical consciousness. Many people do this in landscape – but do not notice. In those
moments she became conscious of her spirituality and the spirituality in all life.)

15 April

(Afternoon) Operation kept to this morning. I think I have the
answer to that which so heavily troubled me the last few days. _

That particular rate of ascension could not carry on accelerating, but had to even out and a form of clarity has appeared which now removes a sort of wide-eyed and egoistic wonderment at it all. That level has been reached – a beautiful initiation into that bizarre knowledge and recognition, and I shall always weep at My Master's presence. But to wander innocently in that Grace is not correct and movement, as a man, must continue to become stronger and *live it* rather than *live with it in wonderment.* I truly hope that this is correct, but the torment of the last 48 hours was horrible and has now worked itself out. But do I really know anything of these things? Am I walking backwards? Truly I trust not, but we shall see. As always, God willing.

And am I beginning to understand the bizarre and unique act of Jesus Christ and how He was like no other Prophet? INRI. As the veils part to show more, there is always an infinite increase in that which I *now* do not know. My worthiness, my worthiness? My correctness in all this? And my Vanity and Weakness?

(*Evening*) Operation kept to.

16 April
Operation kept to, but malevolents surrounding me during oration. A difficult time that I must work out for myself and my own *karma*. Vanity, vanity. But I have that vision. Could it really be so? One would die in it!? (Incidentally, writing a book to make money started – fantasy gibberish.)

17 April
Operation kept to. I have now read well into the New Testament and I believe that now I perceive the true Act of Christ Jesus – that the Son of God did die for us. That before His crucifixion man was not able/ready to perceive in his daily consciousness the divinity of his Spirit which can only be realised, released, integrated by living in Christ's body. (A few pointers in this direction came from a horrible book called *The Spear of Destiny*.) Was this, then, the significant heralding of the Piscean Age to know Tiphareth? Does the Aquarian era hold the promise of raising mankind into the Glory of Chesed and Geburah? (*These questions are phrased in the language or jargon of the Kabbalah , the esoteric tradition of Judaism. Part of the Kabbalistic teaching centres upon a tree of life with different paths and spheres representing different aspects of consciousness and creation. Tiphareth, Chesed and Geburah are Hebrew names for three of these*

different spheres of consciousness and I was contemplating here the possibility that humanity as a whole was entering a new state of being in which there was the possibility of balanced compassion.) Whatever the answers, INRI still and must hold the divine Law for now – and ever. And how many of us realise it – let alone aspire to live it? There is a divine and sublime mystery in Christ's death. For the True Man, Communion must be the act of daily life. In Christ is in Heaven. By Him alone (if you understand His Word) do you come to God, even if in subjectivity one has never heard His name, for *In Nobis Regnat Jesus (In Us Rules Christ)* – and this is a living truth. *(By 'Christ' I often meant not the historical figure of Jesus, but a cosmic principle of unconditional love which actively seeks to help all of us. I see this cosmic principle in Krishna and in the Maitreya Buddha, for example, as much as in Jesus Christ.)*

Our visitor and her presence is teaching me many things about leading and watching. She knows not what she does in sleep and her astronome *(dreambody)*, I think, would vampirize one's grace, psychically and sexually. I have, therefore, put up a *(psychic)* protection and look to see if I am able to perceive it in normal daily life. How to help? I do not know. But I learn every day and, hopefully, we are helped. And I further see myself. Truths higher than reality.

As always now, I feel vanity, vanity. Vanity before the Lord and I beg forgiveness.

18 April

(Morning) Shortly after I went to sleep last night, I was attacked (?) by an astral entity that seemed to try to enter my body – a feeling of suffocation and smothering. I was not frightened for one second and dismissed it by affirming my faith in our Lord Christ. However, had I been cooler I would have found out what it was. I wonder whether it is in any way linked with our guest, but I *very carefully (psychically)* sealed her room last night – I do not know. Or was it purely a test on me or something I alone attracted? Somehow I do not feel that it was dangerous – more lost and sad – perhaps I should have been gentler with it.

(Evening) Operation kept to. Another change is happening, something that makes me nervous. Two things: firstly a strange feeling of great strength which I see could be used for Evil – perhaps, a true Knowledge of good and evil. One must truly know and reject it to have power over it to progress – and it tries to tempt me and then

blackmail me by trying to terrify me into joining it. (If you can't beat it, join it and have a glorious evil time. Temptation, oh Faust, I understand and feel for you.) And I pray to the Saints and my Master for strength and protection. Secondly: a breakthrough in vanity, a dissatisfaction with my body and form; a fearful desire to be truly free of this temporary and unsatisfactory resting-place. A fearful feeling, as I am weak.

19 April

Before going to sleep last night, I clearly saw, with my eyes open and shut, an astronome – shimmering luminous silver molecules. I could not communicate with it; was I too fast or the astronome not psychic? It did not seem at all malevolent – in fact, sadly lost. It went away. I put an odic *(pure energy)* curtain over Frances and myself, and we slept well and easily.

Today I found the blue amethyst for which I have searched. Vanity? It coincides with realizing a few days ago that I possess the twenty-two privileges (except two – one belonging to animals and one to do with resuscitating the dead – unless they are both metaphorical, which may be) that belong to the Adept Magician. I am almost impressed but His Glory shames me and I am sick in His love and my unworthiness. But I feel stronger. I am intending to fast on carrots and bread for the four days of Easter (And Frances, although she may not understand it, is my God-sent comfort).

Operation kept to.

20 April

Operation kept to. *(Referring to the visit of the astral entity)* Nothing last night (but set up strong odic curtain against guest-room.) I still do not know about it.

21 April

Operation kept to. We visited a local town today for a holy day. A pleasant surprise as I met a brother very briefly. In a large crowd, we walked past each other for a couple of yards, then stopped, turned, shook hands and very beautifully acknowledged each other. (I saw him exactly – but not, I think, he me??) Whatever, it was pleasant to be recognised in that magical environment.

I have kept to the fast for Easter. I feel my Master's presence ever closer, but I am neither strong nor worthy enough.

22 April

Operation kept to. I felt Him stronger and closer and was terrified. It was almost completely dark and pouring with rain when I had finished praying, and I felt myself being beckoned back to the Oratory. Like a naughty, bewildered and guilty child, I slunk away – and now, four hours later, I feel those same emotions.

23 April

This morning, lighting the fire, the smoke would not go up the chimney. For the first time I operated the Great Arcanum. The smoke went up. Praise to Him. The fasting must have helped. *(The Great Arcanum is the name sometimes given to the magical method of effecting physical changes psychically using a technique that mixes breathwork with imagination.)*

Operation kept to. Sudden change in stars this evening (coinciding with end of fast).

24 April

(Morning) What I thought to be a sudden change in the stars last night turned out to be something else. As I slept, I was shown into a room where I was pleasantly greeted by two men who said they were brothers, one tall and very strong with a goatee beard, the other Adolf Hitler himself. They said they were glad I was doing work in their direction and would be pleased to give me some first-hand information – and experience. Suddenly their whole tone changed to something totally malevolent and evil – an evil that I have never previously known. They joined hands and I calmly closed my eyes and set up an odic barrier between us, but it was ineffectual. My body quivered from an evil negative electric charge from them and I lost total control. My body in pain from their negative electricity, I was picked up and manoeuvred like a paper doll, completely at their whim. I was totally and vulnerably powerless. Before I returned to my sleeping body, I was temporarily freed from them and found myself looking through a dirty cracked window down at a back-yard (I shall always remember that sight). I came to in my body, sweating, still in some pain and frightened.

Pentagrams, odic barriers were of no use against this power of evil. I then knew that I should not have reacted passively to them, but should have gone into immediate attack. I felt a great failure and immediately, gritting my psychic teeth, attempted to regain contact. I *was not* going to be frightened by them. I gained semi-contact but they were very elusive. I dared them to reappear to do battle, but to no avail. I then brought myself to consciousness. The bedroom was filled with the most malevolent threat and for a few seconds I was *almost* uncontrollably frightened. There was no protection that I could put up except my faith in Our Lord. I picked up the Bible and lit the torch; the light flickered and wavered uncontrollably and I put it out to face them in the dark. Was it Lucifer himself with whom I was in contact? I kept calm as best I could while I was threatened. (Words cannot express that presence of evil.) This would happen again and again, I was told. I would be turned into a quivering wreck of nothingness. Never, I replied. Let it happen for a million years if it means that I may finally be my Lord's servant. I thought of the twelve labours of Hercules. You may have all power on Earth, I was told, and never be frightened and so hurt again. Your power is as nothing to the Lord's, I told them, pitying them as they shrank from His great and wondrous light. I lectured them on their position and work and reminded them of their proper place, finally praying unto the Lord to let His justice and mercy shine on them. Where are you, my Angels, I cried, to protect this servant?

And finally after three-quarters-of-an-hour's battle, they came to relieve me. And I thanked them *greatly*. (And I understood how those great men of evil joined truly the legion after their incarnate death.) Then was I surrounded by a misty vision of a wonderful fraternity of Christian knights and I put on His holy armour to go and do battle. The rest I would not write of. In my vanity, I was at the time and still am amazed at my courage. All power and glory to Him. I have passed one test, a test of deliverance – and what will frighten me now? Again and again, all Power and Glory to Our Lord.

(Afternoon) Both our visitor and Frances had very bad nights, Frances especially. I wonder if I would have survived the night without her? My feelings about last night are changing. Was it such a glorious victory? Was it only what I merit? – a nightmare to teach me a lesson, all the rest just a subjective embellishment? I must hold myself very closely and be ever watchful. I feel my attitude to the Operation temporarily weakening, as though my oration will lose all sincerity. I must hold together, but just at this moment it seems very hard. As always, the Ching advises and corrects me. Oh, I feel so much the worm wallowing in the dung-

heap today. I feel dry, with only my will to carry me through. Suddenly, despite all the great things that have happened, it all seems truly difficult. A dried-out emptiness. Very heavy. I must rest and become calm and strong. So many of the fantasy comforts suddenly appeal to me. And I need, in my weakness, that smile again. Again, this is very heavy. Operation kept to.

25 April

Recovered, partly due to discovering Alice Bailey's Tibetan. (*This refers to the Tibetan teacher Djwahl Khul who wrote many books using Alice Bailey as his secretary.*) Also the I Ching who confirms the future. Unworthiness, discipline, unworthiness. Operation kept to.

26 April

A very tight time of lessons and more lessons. For daylight, for daylight – when worthy. Operation kept to.

27 April

Operation kept to. A bizarre time of great learning, through the courtesy of Alice Bailey's beautiful Tibetan whose tone, wisdom and kindness dwarf all other books that have come my way. Naughtily, I am suddenly quite gleeful – more calm than before. I suppose the whole period started four days ago after the attack in which I think they attempted to kill me (the electric shock). But as ever I must be careful with myself. The whole mystical concept of the Great Arcanum becomes clear – did I understand it before? And there are things – in knowledge, understanding and my future – that I am not writing here. Why? Firstly, it may prove dangerous. Secondly, blasphemous (i.e., what is esoteric *is* esoteric). Thirdly, I may be wrong. And since I began this diary, there are things that I have not written in it. Rightness? The future? The triangle with the cross and diamond. The work. (*I do not remember what I was referring to here.*)

As always into eternity. His Will, Glory and Love. My unworthiness.

28 April

Operation kept to. The Tibetan has really set the ball rolling – in many ways. A clearer understanding, some proper terms of reference. The aspiring mystic becomes the mystic occultist working positively His plan. And I, while undertaking the Operation, am now going to enter into intuitive contact with my brothers. Will action and thoughts along this line hurt the Operation?

I feel as though another attack might occur. I fear it, yet would welcome it if it means another step, another strength. This morning, approached, perhaps even entered, *Samadhi* – or some completely new state of consciousness. Tried again to reach it with *negative* results. The fourth voice cracking through. Our guest leaving today, with practical complications, which have added to the murky energy. She, however, has been initiated. (Also, a perfect case of sacral/throat malfunction which we hope will clear up.) A busy, busy time. Now for some passive re-orientation of everything. Except His Glory and my unworthiness.

I have just re-read the last three weeks and a strange, strange feeling over which part of me writes this. I am watching all this even now. I must somehow crack through and create the one. (How strange that E. *(Edward Glover, my psychoanalyst)* should have said true sophistication is reached when three voices are heard in the head – is this even a fourth?) I must have some peace to move forward with all this new stuff. So much confusion – unless I am holding myself back from the truth and realization. But I fear vanity. I am at the centre of the balance and can see in no direction. Daylight. Daylight.

29 April
Operation kept to. Guest departed yesterday. Highly exhausted and stupid. A time of reflection.

30 April
Operation kept to. Also am working for Paris. *(I was praying and creating thoughtforms to try and dissuade the French government from continuing with surface nuclear testing.)* At 5.10 pm prayed and made contact. Asked if anyone else was working similarly. Received a reply that a brother in Zurich was. Suggested a spiral but lost contact. Is this, I seriously wonder, truth in telepathy or purely subjective naivety? I just do not know and wonder if I am making a fool of myself. But I follow the whims received in me from elsewhere. This whim (??) says also that I have made contact with M. *(I was referring to the teacher known as Maitreya)* in the Oratory, receiving instructions, advice, encouragement, *acceptance* and commitment. This is all truly somewhat boggling to me. I am sceptical,

yet act and feel on it. In the last analysis – today – I place my trust and love in Our Lord – and if the rest accommodates itself to that Glory, then... well, what can I say? Really. My feet on the ground, my head still in clouds trying to make through to Heaven.

For His Glory.

1 May

May Day. Operation kept to. Beautiful – Frances has initiated herself up a grade and now taking sword in her hand; coincides with her having a vision of the magic of her (and the Lord) creating a child, a holy child. Much jubilation in my heart at all this – but ever the fight, for both of us. I shall watch over her with much interest, and love and care as usual. The further she moves, the more she brings the *Shekinah* (*the Hebrew word for a female aspect of divinity that overlights holy occasions and is like Grace or Sophia*) into us, making the earth better and Our Lord joyful.

Myself, I am totally exhausted. I want to sleep and sleep. I want my head through the clouds and in the sky, but there is nothing I can do at the moment, except be watchful of myself. Which, I suppose, is what I am meant to do at the moment. But I have no energy. And I am getting closer and closer, but cannot stretch forth and reach it. Whose blame is this except mine? I have a terrible vain thought that I *cannot* go any faster; if I did, I would disintegrate and lose everything. I want *Samadhi*. (*A meditative consciousness which mixes a completely silent mind with bliss and knowing.*) I want only not to sin against Him – as I do always. Though I fear Him terribly, I feel his Mercy, Pity and Love. And to Him All Glory.

2 May

Operation kept to. Last night very heavy. My astral-emotional (*body*) intensely fighting for control. Things calmer now before I go to bed, but I feel like a battlefield. God willing, the last battle of this kind. How much more of this remains in me? Unworthiness.

3 May

Operation kept to. A morning of great calm, a revelation about being on the Earth, of walking heavily upon His footstool – a bizarre and divine concept, now a reality for me. This afternoon the battle recommenced. Am scarred and very weary, very naughty. Then, in the Oratory this evening, a great and horrible malevolent. With love and *help*, dismissed. That help spoke longer to me with loving and comforting words. Physically, the top of my head is popping in that place – never before so intense.

Frances really and truly initiated into fighting along the path. Good and correct. My protection. How formidable it all (we two) shall be.

As ever, my unworthiness and sins before Him – His Glory.

(Oh, and last night awoke to find myself floating weightless in space and free. Ten seconds later, the unusualness brought me back to earth and my body.)

4 May

My head is popping continuously and quite intensely (at times almost unbearably). I am relatively excited as I know this means a flowing of energy to the pineal and pituitary which might give me full psychism and third-eye vision. We shall see. Last night the popping moved back a few inches from the centre (at the top) of my skull, but has now returned to dead centre. I wonder if those exercises I was instructed to do some time ago have helped or whether it is happening too fast. *(In my meditations some months previously I had telepathically received guidance on how to feel certain energies moving up my spine and through my head, and then back again.)* But my brain seems in good working order. With the help of the *Zohar (this is one of the key books of the kabbalistic tradition)* I think that I may have fathomed one of the secrets of night which will remove all final fear of illusory darkness. Half-an-hour's *(psychic)* exercise to remove toothache. My head well and truly in the clouds, a battlefield again. Very, very hard. My last drop of will to pray in concentration. Operation kept to.

5 May

Physically, mentally and psychically wrecked. My head in storm clouds. Am now calm, but the despair was deep and His *presence* terrified me. Now calm. The battle continues. I shall win. (I think – when? – God willing.) Operation kept to.

6 May

Ill today, but now almost better. Have never previously been so weak. Must calm and continue gently. My oration feeble. Head-popping stopped yesterday; re-started more quietly today. Operation kept to.

7 May

Strength slowly coming back. Frances charging forward. Occasionally this evening I have felt a burning sensation added to the
intermittent throb at the top of my head. Operation kept to.

8 May

Twenty-four hours' calm and rest, and now the battle has recommenced. I must calm and go more slowly with quiet patient
devotion. I think this is the answer, but even as I have approached
that way of behaving, the battle and strain has intensified. Ah well,
four more months to work out the way for Our Lord and an infinity
afterwards in continuation.

Operation kept to.

9 May

Although the battle continues in earnest, for some reason this
evening is somewhat light-hearted. According to the Tibetan's
'esoteric healing' I interpret my head-popping as a setting into
action of the thousand-petalled lotus which indicates the Third
Initiation. Some happiness over this, not that I truly understand it.
*(By this time I was beginning to understand the spiritual path as a series
of initiations, each one marking a new expansion in consciousness and a
greater surrender to Love. In the scheme to which I was attached - and in
esoteric literature there are many different schemes - there is a long period
of discipleship and the proving of real devotion and intention before the
different initiations are possible.)* The one part of it that I can almost
clearly picture is the surge of loving that might be unleashed from
the third eye. Incidentally, am now three-quarters through Vol-
ume 2 of the *Zohar* - a beautiful mystical book with many allusions
that I fail to comprehend. I do, however, understand the vanity
and poverty of those occultists and mystics moving around as
grand masters. A joke on this for Frances. 'If only they/everyone
realised that that halo which they aim for and covet so much is no
more than a sixty-pound crash-helmet crashing around on the
next level up.'

This is all too light-hearted. The battle to be worthy to do His
work, to merely have the right to truly love Him, continues
infinitely with pain (which we deserve).

Operation kept to.

10 May

The battle continues (vanity, weakness, unworthiness). Yet again this light-hearted feeling this evening. And a vision of yet greater strength. Also, my oration must become more joyful. Frances a true comfort as my brain scrambles, really a pillar without whom there might be total collapse. Am beginning to try to interpret my dreams correctly. Head-popping intense tonight. Operation kept to.

11 May

Things happening during oration about which I cannot write. My head torn between complete madness as a veil thrown up to deceive me and a faith in the shock that it really happens. Whichever, it tears me apart and I have seen the Phoenix rising from the weeping ashes.

(It was at this point that I began intensely to experience the real duality within myself. On the one side there was all of me that I had believed to be real – my identity as created within my family, my schooling and my culture; everything that I had identified myself as for twenty years. And on the other side, there was this inner witness, watching, powerful and full of care, with whom I was increasingly identifying. Yet as this realignment took place, it did not feel internally like a graceful shift. It was as if all my internal psychic energies were changing gear but there was no clutch to ease the transition, only a shrill feeling of crunching metal. It gave me headaches and terrible anxiety in my stomach and chest. My old personality instinctively resisted its new position subservient to my identification with my true inner self. At the same time, I was beginning to recognise that I needed, in a dynamic and energetic way, truly to renounce this old personality and that through this renunciation my true Self would be able to. As my true self entered, its energy would alchemically transform my old dying personality and, transformed, it would live again, but now as the metaphorically raised phoenix arising from the ashes.)

Operation kept to. All Glory to the One.

12 May

Life somewhat calmer, but inside the Oratory the same as yesterday continues and a weakness, a fear of sorts, holds me back – I think. I am certain of nothing any more as regards myself and the Path. I understand nothing that is happening within me and to me.

Yet, every day, I see and understand more around me in a very deep fashion. But the ashes. God forbid that it should be the same for all others struggling along the Path, but then, I suppose it must be. If that fight could be lightened for them... And then again, no doubt it has been lightened for me!!! INRI to mention but one.

(I am here interpreting 'Christ reigns within me' as a metaphor for my true Self reigning within me.)

Operation kept to.

13 May

Battle this afternoon. Nightmare of sorts last night again. I did not successfully confront and deal with it while in the dream, but immediately afterwards, feeling the green evil, pulled myself together and was almost instantaneously successful. Again, in the Oratory, great heaviness. To whom am I listening? One separate voice said it was myself. I have no idea what is happening or how I should be reacting.

Wormhood to me. All Glory to the One. Operation kept to.

14 May

In the Oratory this evening, a heavy attack followed by a divine conversation. But was it divine? Are the instructions real or from *me*? Am I totally deluded? We *shall* see. *Ching* unhelpful (me unreceptive?) for a week now – is this part of a ploy? *(I was continuing to throw the* I Ching *for advice but was not now able to make any sense of what I was reading.)* Is all of it a ploy to test my strength and faith (even physically beside me)? I put my faith in Him and no fear will breath my Oath. The confusion is intensely great, but I guard a calm through His Love and Mercy.

Operation kept to.

15 May

The build-up continues. In prayer I feel more effective, closer – I don't know. Operation kept to.

16 May

There is nothing that I may write about today. All Glory to the One.

Operation kept to.

17 May

The voice that I have been hearing is my Teacher's. He spoke with me fully, praising, warning, hinting, so loving. Instructions for and until the climax of the Operation; how to contact him if necessary; how to continue behaving, my future position. Most humble thanks to our Lord, all Glory to the One.

(It was on this day that my intuition that I was being helped by a Teacher on the inner planes grounded in a crystal clear telepathic communication and also in a very real sense of His presence and atmosphere. Part of my training in this period was to distinguish between the energies and intuitions of my own inner self, and the presence and communications of my invisible Teacher. The energy of my Teacher was warm, comforting and very familiar. He also knew me intimately and I felt unconditionally loved and supported by Him. At the same time I felt a responsibility to Him and to His work. I had some images of Him floating in my psyche and they were all associated with the European magical tradition and gnostic Christianity: symbols of the Templar and Rosicrucian orders.)

Now, a time of gentleness and retreat into myself for strength to come. A time of quiet and carefulness.

What can I say? All Glory to the One again and again.

This is one further initiation – like all the others and the ones to come: self-initiation – but with such loving help.

Glory Glory to the One.

Operation kept to.

18 May

And now the battle continues – similar territory, similar tactics, but somehow different. Unworthiness and weakness is ever there before Him, especially so in me. Operation kept to.

19 May

Totally physically wiped out today, cold shivers trying to hold off a fever. Yet, in the middle of this, a long dialogue within, with a suggestion that may re-integrate things: 'I am You are I...' etc. etc. *ad* breaking-point. Oration this evening totally feeble.

Operation kept to.

20 May

Still ill with severe stomach cramp and holding off a fever. Today is the last of the First Two Moons of the Operation and how

wonderful they have been. If I have only lived to be graced with
the knowledge that I have now, to be graced with the ability to
have and perceive His love as I do, I would and do consider myself
the most lucky man alive. Now – to acquire more strength, greater
and deeper knowledge and, mostly, worthiness before Him.
Considering these first two months, I cannot and dare not think of
what may be gained over the next four. The strange miracle is how
Time always passes, with always His teaching so correctly paced.
Lucky and graced am I. All Glory to Him, the One.

The prayer now changes slightly, in that 'before entering the
Oratory ye shall wash your hands and face thoroughly with pure
water. And you shall prolong your prayer with the greatest
possible affection, devotion and submission; humbly entreating
the Lord God that He would deign to command His Holy Angels
to lead you in the True Way, and Wisdom, and Knowledge (by
studying the which assiduously in the Sacred Writings, there will
arise more and more [Wisdom] in your heart).' Also, to fast every
Saturday Eve. My only doubt is in disturbing His Angels, knowing
how hard-worked they are – perhaps there is righteous selfishness
here.

I must repeat my wonder at the end of these two months. From
a dying point of view, it is all too bizarre, too great. But so it is from
any point of view except Above. I thank the Lord for all His
mercies by which *alone* I have been able to tread the Path this far
– and, with His Will, further.

Operation kept to.

THE MIDDLE TWO MONTHS

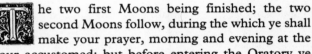he two first Moons being finished; the two second Moons follow, during the which ye shall make your prayer, morning and evening at the hour accustomed; but before entering the Oratory ye shall wash your hands and face thoroughly with pure water. And you shall prolong your prayer with the greatest possible affection, devotion and submission; humbly entreating the Lord God that He would deign to command His Holy Angels to lead you in the true way, and Wisdom, and Knowledge..."

From the instructions of the Sacred Magic
(See pages 69-70 of the facsimile)

21 May

Still ill and very weak and, therefore, in terms of intense energy, an inauspicious start to the second period of two months. However, progress seems to be continuing. I think that my head is now permanently over the clouds – we shall see. I now understand the next step, I think, of making the personality a totally neutral body of energy for use by my soul; it is happening. Deep within, I see again a new strength and another vision. What battles to come to acquire it?

Interesting change in the *Ching*. Over the last two weeks, it has come up three-quarters of the time with 'Youthful Folly' (Hexagram 4) which I finally understand as meaning that I am now big enough to look after myself. Methinks it might give too much credit.

Glory to Our Lord.

Operation kept to.

22 May

Still ill, but just ending I think. Battle continues. Operation kept to.

23 May

Illness going. Battle continues. Operation kept to.

24 May

Illness gone. Feeling stronger. Am also beginning to understand the powers of realization and receptivity that I have – for which all praise and thanks to His mercies. As ever, my terrible unworthiness before Him. Operation kept to.

25 May

I have learnt a great deal about prayer from the *Zohar*, especially in reference to the Psalms. Today I discovered in reality the most recondite mystery of 'Jehovah Elohim'. *(I do not recall what I meant by this.)*

Many things happening today, a *(psychic)* war of sorts, and I thank His mercy for His Messenger. I shall write more fully about this in a few days' time. Psalms 91 and 11.

Operation kept to.

26 May

I feel that the *(psychic)* war is continuing, 'coinciding' with the most extreme day in world news for a long time: Iceland attacks Britain; Argentina change of government and riots expected from terrorists; Greek ship's captain (military) and some crew seek political asylum in Italy; new government in Jordan; news of General Amin having massacred 90,000 in Uganda. Sufficient and creates much food for thought and responsibility.

Another interesting topic for comment is conversation with Angels. By the time an adept has reached this stage, he is bizarrely receptive, strong and seeing. Therefore, and considering the certain degree of strain, he is and must be healthily sceptical about any unusualities in his psyche. This obviously leads to some doubt about the conversation. The doubt, I think, must remain as an insurance – for there are too many others who seek to confuse and bring down his ear – but the voice must be followed with a divine trust. And these voices are so overwhelmingly loving. Again, I will elucidate when the next few days are over – presupposing that I gain a clearer picture.

(On this day I had a conversation with what I took to be an Angel. It was reassuring, but I was also very sceptical. It took place during a time of what felt like intense attack by malevolent energies. Unless one has actually experienced one of these situations, seen the peculiar change in light and directly felt the atmosphere as it affects one's mind and tilts one towards lunacy, it is difficult perhaps to believe in these malevolent forces.)

All Glory to the One.

Operation kept to.

27 May

The war is continuing and, I believe, reaching a climax this evening. I find the Tarot cards most useful for extremely recondite problems, especially in giving an explanation for the present situation. All Glory to the One who puts his Hierarchy to my protection with Him as my Rock. A thousand and ten thousand will fall, but not a toe of my foot...

Operation kept to.

28 May

I think and hope that that *(psychic)* war is now over or ending. The
last four days have been the most threatening and heavy that I
have yet experienced. At points yesterday I thought about being
on the verge of cracking but was saved by the thought: a million
years of this, yes, if it will bring me to Him. The night of 25 May an
Angel came to me in the Oratory and said that he had been sent to
protect me. He was truly most loving and kind and, without his
presence, I dread to think how I would have fared. His interest in
me, however, was not personal but in terms of the *(divine)* Plan. It
seemed a natural enough sequence of events that my (or anyone's)
initiation to this space should set the Black Forces rumbling –
especially considering the outcome of the Operation, God willing.
I remained untouched except for two or three occasions (last night
was very bad with a deep and heavy sweating in the Oratory and
a shimmering Astral all round the house at night), but the rumbling certainly affected our globe, and is continuing. I thank God
for His infinite mercy in protecting me and for sending His
Messenger whom I also thank in deepest affection. God will that
this particular period is over. It has been very difficult, but with the
help, not impossible. Anything, to come to Him. *(It was at this stage
in the six months that I began to experience the reality of the angelic
realms.)*

This evening again a vision of *Samadhi*, the potential rule of my
over-soul. It will come when I desire and will it every second of my
living life. Be calm, strong and wait.

Truly, truly All Glory to the One who looks kindly upon this
feeble worm.

Operation kept to.

29 May

My Lord, what a bizarre and marvellous day. All day I felt very
guilty, very unmagical, Him not sufficiently in my mind. As
though the last four days had in a way defeated me and that I
wished to see and feel nothing. My actions, though, were in no way
sinful or wicked – except, of course, in separateness – but I felt
sinfully empty. My oration this evening took that form – great
guilt before Him – and then...

A vision and feeling of such bliss and graceful strength, a
true baptism of fire. There are no words to describe its wonder, but
such vision. Oh World, the Great Glory of Our Lord should make
us all rise to sing Glory Glory. The Lord Our God is the One God,

loving and merciful, holding everything in Grace and Severity within Him.

This is what the last four days have led to. Four days! A million years. That I should have lived only for this. My Lord, such divine mercy. Now, more work to effect this initiation (initiation is nothing but greater love), to live this space and to make myself truly worthy of this knowledge and strength. To lose all weakness and separateness, for I am still the worm in the dung-heap.

All Glory to Him.

Though out of the Oratory, I am heavily awed and nervous almost, but feel strangely sober.

Operation kept to.

30 May

Today I feel obstructed by myself. Same feelings of guilt as yesterday. Weakness as ever. Operation kept to.

31 May

Still not correct. Operation kept to.

1 June

Everything coming back together. A day of great ease and calm. Everything settled. But I do not lose sight of my poverty. Yes, this time must be used vigorously and usefully. How long may it last? A few days – forever? Operation kept to.

2 June

Ill again – my fault. What a total foolish pathetic waste.

Operation kept to.

3 June

Stupidly, still ill but some joy this evening as Frances had the vision that will see her through the First Initiation. It will be interesting and fun to watch her seeing how it works gracefully through time and not in instantaneous leaps, though the vision *is* instantaneous and all-important. How merciful and great Our Lord is. (*According to my map, at this first initiation, the energy of the heart spins into radiant activity and radiates love whatever the activity of the individual.*)

Operation kept to.

4 June

Considering the atmosphere, it is not surprising that an unwanted visitor has arrived – but he is sent for more work. *(This was a casual acquaintance from London who was passing through Morocco and had managed to get hold of our address.)* I am having to adjust severely to know how to deal with him, but I already think things will happen. Unfortunately, I did not do two hours' reading tonight, but I do consider him as work: am I correct or slovenly?

    Operation kept to.

5 June

Last night was totally disorientated. For the first time I was put off-centre in my weakness and spent the whole night being hauled across the coals – complete and total shame. *(I was now becoming increasingly conscious of myself whilst asleep and apparently dreaming. In this state dreams, imagination and reality merge into a single experience; psychological and psychic struggles become explicit conflicts that are actually lived out and experienced in the dream state. So while being in a dream or a nightmare, I was also self-aware and conscious of how and why I was in the experience. So, for example, if an aspect of my personality was rebelling against the discipline and surrender of the ritual , I would not simply feel uncomfortable and depressed – I would experience this aspect of myself externalised as a figure or a scenario in my dreams and actually enter into struggle with it. At the same time it always seemed as if other energies were attracted to the scene and I had also to deal with them.)* Today more calm but only after a fight.

    This evening, however, a new vision in the Oratory – a sadness of ourselves and energies that gives a bizarre vision and *seeing* eyes. Oh Lord, yet more to live to and I can almost grasp it – if I be worthy. I cannot express the surging feeling I now know. This diary will end when I *am* it. Glory to the One.

    Operation kept to.

6 June

A difficult day. My disorientation over wishing to help our guest helped create a situation that was tearing me apart. Dear Lord, for total tranquillity – though all comes from Him, does it not? More success this evening, the *Zohar* finished, and I am grateful for what it has taught me about prayer. Now reading the *Tibetan Book of the Great Liberation*.

    Operation kept to.

7 June

The last few days have disorientated me very much. I am exhausted and very, very confused. I am unable to see all that has happened clearly and feel as though I am simultaneously walking backwards into the dung-heap and upwards into something I do not comprehend. I cannot judge anything and have felt great, great pain. It is all quite indescribable. In effect, although the external 'circumstances' were uncontrollable, nothing happened except correctly and under will. Perhaps it is only that strain. *(I am referring here to the ongoing sense of tension created by the spiritual struggle, a sense of both the physical tension and of the struggle to hold off nervous collapse and mental breakdown. Mystics deliberately invoke these tensions which then facilitate and provoke inner transformation.)* Today, I know nothing. Everything magically worked, but a feeling of frenetically unworthy emptiness and lowliness. For peace... to pull this mess together.

All Glory to Him for His Mercy and Wonders.

Operation kept to.

An afterthought: My lower self now behaves quite properly and powerfully and is not naughty. My higher self says, 'What on earth should I have to do with this scene?' Quite correct.

8 June

My magic is still lost. Both tonight and yesterday there has been heavy interference in the Oratory but I cope much better and more strongly. Tonight extremely heavy, but I continued in a semi-delirious state. I find that forcing 'them' *(malevolent energies)* to sing psalms with me helps. They left and then a Messenger came who taught me how clumsily I behave, how rude and boorish I am. I might be the most polite man on earth . . . I was filled with much shame. *(This Messenger was an angelic being. My Master had advice for me, but obviously did not have the time to hang around waiting for me to be in a right frame of awareness to receive his advice. He would therefore think his counsel into a cloud of thought energy and give it to the angel who would then hover around me until I was ready to anchor it in brain consciousness. This particular angel was also a sophisticated consciousness in its own right with much experience of working with and helping spiritual aspirants who were specifically on the occult path.)*

I have no excuses today – only dung-heap – and I shall be more watchful. This is a bad and unworthy time, but let me be joyful for the fact that it is occurring in a separate place. *(By much of this, I am really simply saying that I was in an uncontrollably bad mood.)* The New Messenger says he will return as often as is needed.

Glory to the One.

Operation kept to.

9 June

A great battle today to regain normality. With much heavy depression, succeeded more or less (!) in afternoon. In Oratory was again surrounded by the 'heavies' who as usual quite disorientated me and I called them to prayer. The Messenger then returned and explained that I should lower my head in prayer and leave my body vulnerable to them, which I did. A most wonderful lesson in strength, though initially nerve-racking; to be continued. *(I learnt years later that most of the experience of fear is located in the physical/etheric body and it is only after the body has felt this unpleasant energy field that the mind engages. The trick then, when working with these kinds of energies, is to keep the mind disengaged even though the body is experiencing the threat. After a while of working in this way even the body becomes accustomed to the unusual or frightening energy fields and no longer reacts in a fearful mode –simply registering the occurrence.)* Then, again, that vision of *Samadhi* which gives me so much shame yet desire. (My head has begun popping again – I do not understand.)

Operation kept to.

10 June

Despite arrival of Frances' friend, things quieter.

Operation kept to.

11 June

Last night I learnt that an old friend, a potential brother, was obsessed by negative voices. *(I was told that an old friend had displayed schizophrenic behaviour and had ended up under sedation in a mental hospital. He had specifically claimed that he was under attack from demonic forces.)* I prayed for him and told the entity to take me on instead. In bed alone, it appeared, savage and unusually unpleasant and relatively mindless. To commence with I was very, very nervous at its strength, but I later became very sympathetic. I called down the Messenger and asked if He could remove it. 'To where,' he replied and then said that I could only do so by dissolving and absorbing it in my own love. I do not feel able to do that at the moment, but hope that I shall after the Operation. A most glorious day today. In the oration, I achieved Unity, *Samadhi*, no words to describe it. And I held it for many minutes, even for a while outside. Oh, for it permanently to be free and serve. Mouni Sadhu's *Samadhi* says one cannot hold it permanently – that is too heavy a goal, but I wonder... (*I was finally coming into the meditative experience of complete unity with all life whilst experiencing bliss.*)

I wonder more and more about this Operation. At the beginning, I felt it to be more than that which appeared. Certainly, the occultists have little idea about it at all.

I am nervous tonight and somewhat overcome. The duality after the Oneness with its remembrance is very hard.

Am naughty in that I stopped reading *The Tibetan Book of the Dead* half-way through to read Alice Bailey's *From Bethlehem to Calvary*, meanwhile dipping into Mouni Sadhu.

All Glory to the One and all thanks to His Angels for I remain a worm – but a worm that glows somewhat. Operation kept to.

12 June

Yesterday still echoing, effecting through me. Today I realise increasingly its import and there are no words... though the writers whom I am currently reading attempt to verbalize, at times approaching its vision and transcendence. This, I think, is the true Third Initiation according to the Tibetan. (*According to this particular initiatory map, the third initiation is when the personality becomes fully open to the energy and awareness of the soul which explosively radiates outwards transfiguring the whole personality.*) Who knows? Yesterday, after which no sensation, knowledge or consciousness will be the same. All is changed – not a stupefying flash, but a calm Oneness – a dissolution in Him. There can be *no* slipping back now. Everything is confirmed and cemented in His One Total Love and Transcendence. That despite my unworthiness this should have been granted... Operation kept to.

13 June

The change continues. Operation kept to.

14 June

The change still continues with a crisis today as I realized the horror of the duality. Constant conversation between the two – in reality – coaxing, imploring, telling-off, loving. This must be

worked out shortly or I shall crack in my sickness in His love.
Operation kept to.

Have read Alice Bailey's *From Bethlehem to Calvary*. Now reading *The Mysteries of Chartres Cathedral*.

15 June

In the Oratory this evening, am tortured and scarred and I understand little of all this. It is a quite ravaging and breaking experience
that totally crushes me at the time. I almost walk to my oration now
in a fearful state, ready for that war. It is deserved and will take me
further. *(My personality resistance to the discipline and surrender was
now extraordinarily intense.)* But I cannot express its heaviness. Am
reminded of the phrase, 'the dark night of the soul', but I feel that
that is truly yet to come.

A balancing bit of pathly happiness comes from a sudden
understanding of the Temple below and the Temple above. *(Reading the book on Chartres Cathedral I had begun to experience how my own
body and personality vehicle was a reflection of the divine heavenly body.
The correspondence between the two created the possibility of the little
human vehicle vibrating in total harmony with the greater heavenly
vehicle and thus bestowing a magical blessing on the world around.)* I
must see if I can truly learn to *understand and know* their process of
functioning.

Did not read for two hours this evening.
Operation kept to.

16 June

Calm as I write this, but a most heavy battle again today. A feeling
of total loss, aimlessness, some aloneness. And that part of me –
me/I – that I – which I? – am attempting to draw up forever into
that light, screams and screams like a lost child in the desert that
never ends, in which nothing can be sensed or perceived. It clings
desperately to this life. I do. Which I? – melodramatic? Perhaps in
this moment of calm, but in the Oratory the battle is severe. All it
tells me is that I am a sinner. Nothing will stop me continuing and
I know too well how much this is required, is my due, in fact
everyman's who stumbles along the Path. How long, though?
And what can I do? Here, for the first time, rigid discipline and my
powers are of no help or use. The very essence is shaking. As it well
might...

The Lord protects me through it, ever Merciful in His Judgement. Operation kept to. *Chartres* book finished and I have a clearer vision of future work and its practicalities. Yes? All *will* be well?

17 June

A slight problem, as our guest is totally functioning in her emotional body, with orientated flights into mental, and is a grey cloud in our midst. There appears to be no way of helping to raise her in any way as there is heavy suppressed hostility. It is very sad and like so many others. I suppose this is a test of harmlessness and pearls before swine. I see no way at all around it. Is this so much my fault?

The battle continues, but slightly less intense.

Operation kept to.

18 June

It all continues. Am now reading Mouni Sadhu's *Samadhi*, which is very helpful. Along with honourable advice from Ching, it would seem that a change of attitude is in order: the outcome of the struggle is inevitable. Since childhood I have known this future – therefore do not fight, but use joyful calm. I do not think, however, that I can do that; the outcome is inevitable but 'heaven must be stormed'.

I do not know.

Operation kept to.

19 June

It continues still. Having left the Oratory this evening, I was called back in to confront a real 'heavy' with whom I dealt by having it recite the Lords's Prayer with me. It did not bother me as it is in fantasy compared to what I am going through at the moment. To be quite honest with this diary, I do not wish this state to continue or happen ever again. It is unbelievably tortuous and painful. Truly, the only strength is in Him at the moment. If this is not 'the dark night of the soul', and that is yet to come... But Faith, Hope and their protection will see one through everything. And I know the inevitability of the future. So whatever must, obviously must – and with a good heart... But it *is* so heavy and I bleed for the others. *(Other mystics who follow this path.)*

Operation kept to.

20 June

It still continues. Heavier and heavier. My only solace is in the thought that it will end in a month or so and then the light. God willing. Operation kept to.

21 June

Summer solstice.

It still continues, plus horrible stomach cramps over the last few days. I have suddenly become very aware in reality of the astro-mental energies emanating from me and I am trying to place it under total discipline, occasionally ensuring that nothing at all emanates. *(I learnt during that time of the absolute reality that people vibrate or radiate or emanate their emotions and thoughts into the environment. Since then I have been an exponent of 'spiritual ecology', the recognition that our ecological responsibility includes the discipline of cleaning up our emotions and thoughts in order not to further pollute the atmosphere.)* At the same time this takes the workability of the Great Arcanum to its limit and gives me an awful assessment of my power in terms of creation and action – it is quite the most extreme 'weapon' or creative ability a man may possess. I pray the Lord that I am acting through this period as I should, but I am truly learning all that is and is to be sacrificed. I welcome it and am disgusted at my previous non-understanding of these basic truths and my current fleshly resistance. More and more I know what I am to be which gives me even greater shame at what I have been and am. And, in time, every man and living thing shall enter that consciousness of Him.

Again, it continues and I am overcome with pain and shame, and sick in His love for my sinfulness. I am nothing.

Operation kept to.

22 June

And heavier. Oi. I do not think that I am bearing up to it or behaving well. Total resistance, friction. No words, am just waiting. Operation kept to.

23 June

It continues still. Not to be shallow, there is always someone worse off. Today I saw the actual sacrifice of our Mother Earth, and how she must rise with us – or that we must take her and everything with us. And today she gave me great comfort. Have finished

Mouni Sadhu's *Samadhi* and am now reading D.K.'s *A Treatise on Cosmic Fire*, ninety per cent of which I do not understand. (Also am stopping cigarette smoking which adds to the strain.)
Operation kept to.

24 June

Today takes the prize as the most heavy, disorientated and tortuous yet. Everything is flowing, shrieking out (aided by nicotine withdrawal symptoms, after thirty a day for ten years). To put it bluntly, was pretty freaked. Another 'heavy' in the Oratory who had me sweating and accelerating the prayers to get out. But – a vision that if I really 'heavy' it, I'll burn my way through, and this gives a slight ray of light at the end of this horrible but deserved tunnel. I am not aiming too high, but how low am I? Understand hardly anything in *Cosmic Fire*, will read it twice. Really the extremity of today has surprised me. What is yet to come?
Operation kept to.

25 June

I think that this particular period may be coming to an end. The oration this evening was much calmer, but things happening, rods, etc., that may be total hallucinatory and suggestive fantasy. *(By 'rods' I was referring to the rods of initiation, or intensely channelled energy, that great Teachers use to stimulate their students' energy and help them through initiation.)* It may be otherwise, but I feel that I know nothing and am worthy of nothing.
Operation kept to.

26 June

Yes, these horrible days are ending and I am re-emerging, but with a full view of all that needs doing. No doubt a similar period will recur before the end. All of the last ten days, following the one which achieved/showed *Samadhi*, have truly demonstrated to me the work that must now be done and I am gradually preparing myself for this war, reckoning to put the whip fully across me as I begin the last two months (years?!) on 21 July.

I feel at the moment that I am a lazy, unworthy sluggard, but I must, I think, approach the coming war with full and calm preparation.

Do I now see a hazy glow at the end of the tunnel? Perhaps, but I do not deserve to – and all is vanity.

Today Frances took up the sword to charge (stumble) forward like all of us. God with her along the thorny path as she storms Heaven.

Operation kept to.

27 June

The bad period definitely over – temporarily – and now a time of growth again. A vision of living a new consciousness. In the Oratory, I feel that Unity will reign supreme over the duality and I am no longer so pained by it as I see hope – indeed a glow at the end of the tunnel. But I must prepare carefully for that war, though diplomatic relations are already being strained prior to full declaration. *Cosmic Fire* now in parts understandable, but sparking me into a greater understanding and wisdom of the Unity and the Whole Plan. Perhaps I know absolutely nothing – nothing at all from my wormly state. (But, obviously, life is better.)

Operation kept to.

28 June

Tonight in the Oratory my lower mental faculty *(the chattering mind)* went temporarily totally out of control and had to be painfully slapped down; its surge of energy was astonishing and made me ever more conscious of what must be done. *But* I came in contact with the *monad*, my over-soul, my spirit – contact only, not unity – and place myself under its instructions, something I *must* do continuously. At this moment, I cannot hold it and, in fact, resist it; *but* I will place myself totally under its control and do *nothing* without its agreement or, to be more exact, its instruction. This is all very difficult, but it is indeed movement for this unworthy worm. Operation kept to. *(According to my map of spiritual consciousness , derived from esoteric Buddhism and theosophy, the psyche has three major aspects: the personality – the soul – and pure spirit, the monad . When the personality has fully opened to the consciousness and energy of the personal inner soul, it is then possible to begin to have contact with pure cosmic spirit, sometimes also called monadic awareness. In my experience, soul awareness was like an ocean of bliss; monadic awareness was like a laser beam of ecstasy opening up into infinity.)*

29 June

I lose the voice. *(By 'voice' here I mean a sense of monadic, pure spirit, awareness.)* I lose it. In the Oratory this evening I regain it and stay in communication for half-an-hour and then I lose it again, using almost any excuse. *(i.e. Any tiny murmuring thought of my mind could distract me.)* I *will* hold it. Perhaps a form of breakthrough with and for Frances this evening, that she should have vision with me (apart from anything else to help me), but I don't think she can hold *that* for long – as me above: joke. *(I drew here in the diary a six pointed star and I have no idea what I thought was a joke.)* Operation kept to. The whip will be applied to take me home, if I be ever worthy.

30 June
No voice today, but perhaps greater control. I don't know. I know nothing at the moment about what is happening or about to happen; equally whether I am behaving correctly or appropriately; equally where all this is leading to. I feel I must hold together and push harder. My head burns occasionally during the oration. *A Treatise on Cosmic Fire* now sparking off many thoughts.

Frances going through a crisis which only worries me in relation to the Last Two Months as I dread the environment that might be created by her interference and my reaction (disappearance) to it. It will all come out though. It does raise interesting problems, having a wife on the Path, and makes it quite difficult at times. I must treat her as a sister, but her hangovers are overpowering sometimes.

Operation kept to.

1 July
Brought almost to snapping-point in the Oratory this evening by noisy dogs, truly to snapping-point – followed by a short flood of feelings about how my personal environment is out only to frustrate this Operation. Now cool, but the situation was such that I realised the actual strain on myself during the orations. Dear Lord, forbid such interference, I beg you.

Frances has reached crisis-point and is freaking out. I must and can only sit back and allow *karma* and the Path to take its due course. If she only had the eyes to see, she'd see my help and true sympathy – but the whole climax and crisis is to gain those eyes and that vision. She will emerge shortly. And me? I know nothing. I am nothing. *(By this stage the strain that I was under was beginning to be felt by Frances. She also was in the disorienting position of being in*

a relationship in which I had suddenly, in a few months, gone from being an interesting and urbane explorer of consciousness to a fanatical occultist/mystic. She was also experiencing the threat of all the malevolent energies. I was incapable at the time of loving properly or of giving her proper care and affection. I saw only the shadow aspect of her behaviour and had no understanding or compassion for her situation.)
Operation kept to.

2 July

For some time now I have been meaning to summarise certain things: feelings or points I forgot to write. Perhaps I do it today because I am sufficiently bored or perhaps it is in the middle of an unknown time.

Firstly, some relatively mundane things. In about the second week of January, Frances and I no longer prayed together; I forgot to mention this, but since that time she has prayed daily on her own, so that is all very good and no worry.

About exteriorising *(going consciously out of my body)*: this has definitely been put off. (*a*) it is not very important; (*b*) at the moment it could prove very dangerous for me because I would come under attack from those forces which will be placed under my authority at the end of the Operation; so (*c*) I should not exteriorise until I have total authority over the Astral's inhabitants. I have done no *(exteriorisation)* exercises at all since beginning the Operation; that would have been too much.

I take everything that is happening and has happened very much for granted. It is only if I calmly look back that I am filled with a wonder at the total coherence of the Path and the track that led to it. We cannot approach understanding God in any way, but I dare to say that I know the Love, Wisdom and Justice of His emanation, that when I finally turned my face, mind and heart to Him, He enveloped me in His energy to show the Path. The way we left home and the way the books were chosen; the way in which we found Here. The way everything was prepared for this Operation; my whole life coming to this exact point. The protection and love shown me; the strength that was given me during the two attempts on my life and the other attacks. One day I will know the past that allows this Present. There have been no teachers, only books and His love, and His Messengers. That I may be so honoured to crawl out of my state by His will.

Also, I must mention the balance of the Occult against the Mysticism. They have walked hand-in-hand, though at this point

I look only to my liberation and what I may then go back to learn. My liberation – is that a reality? Where am I now? I know not. Sometimes I feel that at the end of these six months I will be allowed to start the Path of Aspirants – and, at other times – now – I look to liberation in the full knowledge of its full and heavy meaning. *(By Path of Aspirants I mean the very beginning of a conscious approach to spiritual transformation.)* My own fantasy past makes me look to that End – am I right? I know not. It is all in other hands, is it not?

The Operation itself can, I think, be brought to successful fruition by a disciple of the Third Initiation and, therefore, any initiation above that. I believe that the actual process of it is taking me higher – again, I know not in fact. Through *Cosmic Fire*, I begin to understand the forces that I will be allowed to control; when I began I had no idea at all. If the progress of the last three-and-a-half months is further paralleled, then I may expect great things(?). It goes without saying that I am still an abysmal sinner, in vanity, separateness and self-remembrance. Very occasionally my astral is interferesome; my physical as regards cigarettes (now five a day but none by 21 July) and food; my lower mental more frequently; my higher mental nearly continuously. But my monad is beginning to exert a control that I can consciously feel and sense and this will grow and develop until there is no argument at all – Unity!! God willing. What a joke, though – me! and everything here and that has been previously felt and thought. But then again the unwriteable truths of everything, and responsibility. About these things I shall not write – it is not needed – they are written everywhere in higher languages which one day *all* will understand. There is, however, a great weight in the things that I cannot say, the aloneness of some of it. The vision that cannot be shared though one day *all* will see. But above me is comfort and learning.

For today – I live two lives: one in the Oratory and one outside it. They are totally and completely split. But I feel that they are coming gradually (very gradually) together. Also, now, I am perhaps beginning to reap from all that pain and horror. I might see the end of the tunnel and suddenly I am happy. For how long? Is it reality? Still, I know nothing.

Operation kept to.

3 July

A day of much environmental tension (involving a slight attack on me – slight? Perhaps I know now better how to cope as, in reality, there is little to cope with as my monad is hardly involved in fear); perhaps today an environmental climax. Anyway I am working towards creating calm for the last two months.

Operation kept to.

4 July

(Morning) Am suddenly moved by the thought that as I struggle to release myself totally from all illusion, my life in Maya *(the Hindu word for 'illusion')* during this incarnation has brought me many happy moments – and putting aside the struggle for the Path!! – little pain or sad memories. Strangely, this touches me deeply.

This evening (5 pm) in her exercises, Frances encountered a figure; after certain advice from me, she allowed him to reappear. A Chinese(?) figure, whom I also saw and spoke with shortly. I believe perhaps the Master D.K. himself (??). He came to help Frances get together. He is very beautiful. There is more to this. Whatever, we are all extremely grateful. Frances will change over the next few days or... *(Re-reading this almost two decades later I am surprised by how casually I describe it. Frances suddenly encountered a figure in the garden, a shimmering figure who appeared and then disappeared because of her nervousness. I helped her to relax and feel safe, and the figure reappeared in total clarity before us in the garden. It seemed to be the Tibetan teacher Djwahl Khul. He had come expressly to comfort Frances and to help her deal with the whole situation. He manifested to us for two or three minutes, a calm and loving energy, soothing and healing the situation. He then disappeared into thin air, just as he had manifested in the first place. I felt enormous relief and comfort at his presence. And the situation for Frances began to feel somewhat better.)*

Myself, am still preparing for the coming battle, sharpening weapons, assessing more and more the enemy, myself. Truly, many thanks and blessings.

Operation kept to.

5 July

I noticed very clearly today, by a trip into town, how easy it is for the higher mental observation to be almost totally disorientated – and that is *not* to say that it *is* frequently orientated. It is strange how I approach the last Two Months in a similar fashion to the way in which I approached the beginning of the Operation. But the total peace and stability that is *so* absolutely needed must be prepared for; without that peace (partly environmental, but mainly to do with being *continuously in a state of meditation*), I shall be *foutu. (French vernacular for useless.)* 'Continuously in a state of meditation' is the essential key, powered by intense will, desire and love, that will bring, God willing, liberation. As always, I am currently writing nothing of the spiritual concepts and truths that I am learning: either they cannot or should not be written, or else they have *already* been written elsewhere. Whom do I wish to bore?

One-and-a-half hour's reading only, but six hours yesterday.

Operation kept to.

6 July

The build-up continues, but with it also progress in knowledge, if nothing else. Have finished *Cosmic Fire* which I shall read again with notes, having first re-read *Cosmic Doctrine*. The Master D.K. is truly most beautiful and to Him and His writings I owe much gratitude. My head still burns/pops occasionally: I think this occurs when I am being 'radioactive' as that would be the exit for the re-vamped *prana*. I shall experiment, but I also have a thought – this minute – that I must always or sometimes (which?) use my third eye to direct; this would not seem correct if 'bathing the Mother in Love'; but for other Magic, perhaps most certainly so. *(This is a very obscure passage. I was, in fact, learning how to consciously direct the different energies in my body and also how to radiate these energies into the world around me. I was also learning when it was appropriate simply to surrender myself and bathe my mother – my body – in love.)*

I told Frances what may occur in the future. We shall see. I repeat that I continue preparation for these final Two Moons.

Operation kept to.

7 July

The process continues. Am learning, seeing more. In the Oratory this evening I see how to affect people by communicating directly with their Soul (and perhaps diluting the opposing sheafs *(of their personality vehicles).* Also, something psychic/physical occurred which I do not comprehend; a feeling, never previously experienced, of great heat – I do not know at all – very disorientating, totally shaking *(my body)* but bringing no new opening – similar in novelty to the epileptic fit. But my assessment at the time was disturbed by external noise. Am studying and taking notes from *Cosmic Doctrine* – already seeing somewhat. Operation kept to. (Also at end of oration was visited by 'heavies' who have difficulty now in heavying me. tee hee.) *Thank God.*

P.S. *(Half-an-hour later in bed)* It suddenly truly dawns on me what a beautifully powerful thing I learned today – powerful and capable *only* of great good. All Praise.

8 July

It continues. Today overshadowed by a vow never to smoke another cigarette; the physical-lower-astral reaction is quite amazingly tremendous. I am helped by Frances doing similarly, but fear she'll have a rougher time. Myself, I am truly ashamed, an initiate two-thirds through this Sacred Operation, to be in this situation. *(I am referring here to the business of thinking myself to be an occult initiate, but being in a state because I'm stopping smoking.)*

Operation kept to.

9 July

The preparation continues, but today is totally overshadowed by the lack of nicotine though I don't think this psycho-physical reaction will last long. I did *not*, however, do two hours' reading today as I only pulled myself together this evening, but I did six hours yesterday. Food intake has also been heavily cut down over the last week – no eggs or cheese, hardly any dinner.

Operation kept to.

10 July

(Morning) Last night, through my sleep, amazing things – both feelings *and* concepts – that I hardly remember and fail to grasp now. What stands out most is at one point : standing on the edge of the Universe, feeling *total bliss* and feeling that I, out here, was the creator. I, then (not surprisingly at this time, eh?) was frightened by the sensation and returned outwards to safer ground.

(pm) The rest of today dominated by nicotine withdrawal, climaxing with a stupendous return performance of little Me finally emerging to pathetically protest Frances' horrible behaviour (yes) over last four months. I think that that is the last we have seen of him, but presently and in parallel I despair of Frances in connection with the next two months (see 30 June). If she 'sucks' as I enter

the other state, it will not be good for her – and it seems now that there is nothing that I can do to help and, it must be remembered, a far superior visitor has also been to try and influence with little effect. We shall see. I'm sure it will be all right... *(It is fairly obvious here that I am projecting my difficulties at stopping smoking on to Frances.)*

Operation kept to.

11 July

I hardly wish to write this. Following yesterday, the young master made a tumultuous return performance mainly in the continued face of Frances' obstruction. That *is* definitely his last appearance, but even this shameful period holds its lessons. As regards my wife – this is *magic* – I give it a few more days to see whether it is viable or not. May God forgive this present state. Operation kept to.

12 July

Everything relatively normal, but the preparation continues. Also, much is being learnt and, as I stop to look calmly, I see that this is a fruitful and educatively heavy time, as was the end of April. (I think Frances may be coming under her control – we shall see.) Now I wish to regain my love and calm, and then to be One.

Operation kept to.

13 July

(Morning) A very heavy night last night (!) including a battle with some astral fiend that *was* connected with Frances. It is, I hope, now completely banished. I am totally exhausted, another problem being that with no nicotine and eating less, a supercharge of energy is coming through to me but is not evenly balanced and is concentrating on my sacral centre *(the chakra associated with the reproductive organs.)*. I must find a way of raising it.

(Afternoon) Again, I am struck by what is being learned and felt – sparks covered in a series of sheafs; myself especially, and therefore clearer vision of my 'weakness and wickedness'. I feel, though, that once I'm over this psycho-physical discomfort, the home-run to first base (!!) may begin. This may all be premature but it fills me with anticipatory joy and bliss. (Frances is almost there, but not quite.)

Operation kept to.

14 July

A last-flight lunchtime binge, complete with cigar. Now what can I say? The grating of being torn apart so is quite nerve-racking and of immense strain but not *per se* painful. Not painful, as a glow of light is seen at the end of the tunnel about which I fear to write for fear of dissipating energy that will take me there. But the essence of the matter is that bizarre and continuous meditation that recognizes the 'I' that I am and that sees through the various kernels to ultimately burn through them and transform them into a suitable vehicle. The strain is holding that meditation; the strain is not holding it; it is all strain – but *deserved*, and shortly I shall increase the pressure as much as I can. This gradual approach is, I think, working well. I know nothing. Operation kept to – oh, I am taking a biro and paper to bed with me to jot down things that are happening education-wise if I can be awake sufficiently. The last three nights have been replete with lessons which I absorb(?) but consciously forget. *(Much teaching and education takes place in the dream state; most of it is absorbed and integrated subconsciously; sometimes there is fully conscious awareness of the lessons.)*

15 July

I am really not at all certain what is happening around me and in my reactions. This evening, a concerted environmental symphony to stop my prayer. *(The kind of symphony I am referring to included dogs howling all around, donkeys braying, curious locals walking too close to the oratory and so on; plus a great deal of negativity in the atmosphere; plus my own bad moods.)* Operation kept to.

16 July

The lead-in continues and how tortuous it is; the duality is killing; the threats are heavy. For a few days now I have been meaning to mention something for the sake of someone/anyone into whose hands this diary may fall. Concerning this Operation, it is in human terms the most tough and frightening experience possible; apart from courage, it requires a spiritual intelligence to prevent inevitable self-destruction. If anyone considers performing it, I most heavily advise them to meditate upon it for at least twelve months beforehand before swearing the oath to carry on through it.

As may be gathered, I am finding it heavy going at the moment. I have seen so much (or so little) but am not able to be it, but I must be patient. It is very hard at the moment; from one extreme to the other (in truth). And two months more; ah, I have these two months to do it, God willing. God, what a pathetic creature I am before you.

Operation kept to.

17 July

Today has been too, too horrible; a movie of the worst way I could possibly behave at the moment, culminating in shaving my head. The moon is two days full. It will all pass, but I am filled with pain and most terrible shame. How, knowing all that I know, able of all that I am able, could I descend to behaving like this? No environmental pressure of even the most extreme kind provides an excuse and yet I find myself smiling as I write this. May I be forgiven.

Operation kept to – I should mention the incredible torrent of energy, mostly astralized, that is pouring through me at the moment. No sleep last night or the night before.

Today, a letter sent to J. to initiate him – God willing. (*I believed that a friend of mine was about to enter upon the spiritual path and that my letter to him would help trigger him into taking the first steps.*)

18 July

I think this bad (horrible) time is coming to an end. I shall see. Once it has truly ended and I have found an isle of strength and calm within myself, then I shall push myself really hard. At the moment not all is perfectly under control as it should be and there is, therefore, no point in trying to *push* on and make things/me worse than I am already.

I must mention the swallows in the valley who put on such amazing flights; I am extremely grateful to them for not only have they entertained me with their bizarre aeronautic beauty, but they are the only cosmic physical form to whom I have been able to relate easily and break this aloneness. On the radio last night they have finally found an astronomic Black Hole in space – this, according to the astronomers, does not put paid to the 'big bang' theory but indicates that all universes will be magnetically/gravitationally pulled back within themselves, after which there will be a further 'big bang' and so on *ad infinitum*. Good Heavens!!

May the Lord forgive my vanity and weakness. Truly.

Operation kept to.

19 July

Something that I have not, strangely, mentioned about the last few weeks is that I am totally exhausted, mentally and physically. It is for some form of normality energywise that I am waiting before taking off the brakes – I think?? The other daily syndrome: unity is more of a reality after waking, and duality becomes more apparent and painful as the day goes on – necessarily, through my weakness. Last night, a most beautiful period of supreme transcendence which confirmed all aspirations (this morning I would have said 'knowledge'). In the Oratory this evening, at one point the image of Saturn and the information that I am of the Third Ray – I do not understand or know whether to take seriously.

Frances now setting up protective barriers round house.

Operation kept to.

20 July

(Morning) Tomorrow morning begins the Last Two Moons. I will now pray three times a day: at dawn, before lunch and at sunset. Washing beforehand, I will wear the white linen robes for the orations and the lamp will always be alight, and there will be perfume on the censer. The prayer now changes slightly:

... and firstly ye shall make Confession of all your sins; after this, with a very ardent prayer, ye shall entreat the Lord to accord unto you the particular grace, which is, that you may enjoy and be able to endure the presence and conversation of His Holy Angels, and that He may deign by their intermission to grant unto you the Secret Wisdom, so that you may be able to have dominion over the Spirits and over all creatures...

Also towards the end of your Oration, ye shall pray unto the Holy Angels, supplicating them to bear your sacrifice before the Face of God, in order to intercede for you, and that they shall assist you in all your operations during these two Moons.

You shall shun all society except that of your wife and servants. Ye shall employ the greatest part of your time in speaking of the Law of God, and in reading such works as treat wisely thereof.

(Afternoon) Today has been of a great change – a greater living of the vision; somehow a more certain knowledge of everything. But it is so strange that as I think ahead to that which I sense and will to be the Truth, I am overcome with shame and guilt; I am suddenly afraid of even daring to think of that as possible; I shall be ever punished for contemplating it, sinner that I am, a silk purse

out of a sow's ear?! Even as I remember William at the age of nine in school prayers, knowing himself to be what he now hardly dares to think. Lord, I, this sinner, know nothing; forgive me if my vanity blasphemes you. Part of all this sparked off by the Master D.K.:

'Occult irritation... is friction... the last fetter which the Master casts off is irritation. The personality no longer attracts attention; friction therefore ceases... '

For how long may one be irritated? Weeks, months, years, incarnations? I know nothing.

Operation kept to.

THE FINAL TWO MONTHS

Morning and Noon ye shall wash your hands and your face on entering the Oratory; and firstly ye shall make Confession of all your sins; after this, with a very ardent prayer, ye shall entreat the Lord to accord unto you this particular grace, which is, that you may enjoy and be able to endure the presence and conversation of His Holy Angels, and that He may deign by their intermission to grant unto you the Secret Wisdom, so that you may be able to have dominion over the Spirits and over all creatures.

Ye shall do this same at midday before dining and also in the evening; so that during these last Moons ye shall perform the prayer three times a day...

Furthermore, ye shall have a Vest and Tunic of linen, which ye shall put on every time that ye enter into the Oratory, before ye commence to put Perfume in the Censer..."

From the instructions of the Sacred Magic
(See pages 70-73 of the facsimile.)

21 July

An interesting disorientation, praying at noon as well. Duality
severe. I am not where I have been and that is the knowledge that
meditation must be continuously held. The swallows are swifts:
they are presents and have and are creating much joy and thanks.
(By now my main source of relaxation and amusement was to sit on the
roof of our house and watch the baby swallows being taught how to fly.
They all lived in a nest about ten feet away.)

And now, as four Moons are over and two begin, how can I
begin to thank and wonder at the Lord who has led and protected
me, and whom I, a worm, by the grace of His loving kindness have
dared to address? I? It is very strange sometimes and still with
occasional blatant fear, and much weakness. I dare not know or
think anything, dare I?

Operation kept to.

22 July

I am learning a great deal suddenly and I study and separate I from
I. Though ever a most terrible and awful weak worm before Him.

Operation kept to.

23 July

Everything is calming somewhat, including Frances. The duality
is disappearing slightly as I realize suddenly today that 'I' am the
balance between the personality that was 'William' and the soul or
monad. Which part am I? Not quite certain.

I also know that with this learning and discipline and speed, I
lost sight that all that this allows me to do is to approach and love
God more. I am ever the ungrateful and blind and vain worm.

Operation kept to.

24 July

Screaming duality today caused by my emotional reaction to my wife. But 'I' *(my focus of consciousness)* am here:

perhaps – if I know for certain what the two triangles are and, more exactly, what that point is. However, the upper point is one with whom – when I 'can' or make myself 'listen and hear' – I am commencing a true relationship, and I have begged it, I, to take over. 'How can I?' it replies, 'the vehicle is not ready. Behave and *(put into)* order your astral *(emotional energy)* concerning your wife and immediate environment and perhaps I shall descend.' And then also I, me that is, keep tearing myself over whether that point at the centre of the hexagram is soul, personality, mental unit or what? And whether the voice is objective when depressed? Soul, or when, elated, cocky? I know nothing and am abysmal before Him. It's all this talk of Initiation by the Tibetan whose real name is Master Djwahl Khul. (A joke: William Bloom is dead. Monsieur Whizz-Bang rules instead.) Oh Lord.

Operation kept to. As an addendum, I should note at the moment that I am filled with a supercharge of external energy (almost totally analogous to previous experiences with drug LSD but *no* disorientation).

25 July

The bliss and the horrors. My personality, I think, rules. I vainly thought it was dead. Still, I have a shallow hope that all this horror is not from my personality but elsewhere. I am lost, confused and stupid. I should be worshipping our Lord and thinking of nothing like this, may He forgive me. (Reading *Esoteric Astrology* – understanding very little.) Fantasy land and me. Me!! Who? Oh Lord.

Operation kept to. But it's moving pretty high energy and I am very grateful.

26 July

I continue to *not* understand what is happening. Again, it is the strangest heaviest period ever. It's all, I think to do with wiping out my personality. I think. I know and understand nothing at this moment. But nothing in it worries me. In fact the opposite – though I become hourly more aware of my sinfulness in vanity and arrogance before Him. The oration this evening was strange, but I don't know why. Who am I inviting down? My soul or monad? Why am I so pathetic and weak before Him? Why so many grand words but separatist wanderings? All this – the problem with which we/I (who?) shall deal. Obviously this is all an initiation of sorts – which? I don't know – second, third or fourth. Or first or a quarter. Really, confusion, and I must forget all this and just be a channel for His Love. But the Operation itself is something else: 'Grant unto me O Lord The Secret Wisdom. Deign to let me have Dominion over spirits and all Creatures. Let me enjoy and endure the conversation of the most Holy Angels.'

All by His Will. Two trips? Strength – weakness. I must calm to work this out. I can achieve great calm. But in it I know nothing – though the state is blissful – know nothing of what is happening, but am more sophisticated and wise than ever before. It is all strange. And I am a feeble worm.

Operation kept to.

(An hour and a half later) I think this tawdry period has reached a climax. Something has burst within. Perhaps I am over a hump. (Frances certainly is if she can hold it – which she *will*.) For myself, we shall see tomorrow and shortly I should calmly summarize all that has actually been happening – if I know it!? Thanks and all Praise to Him that He allows we worms to exist.

27 July

A concerted environmental attempt today to totally disrupt the peace by servants, etc., and peace was disrupted for a few hours. *(The local family who cared for the garden, and whose son we employed to help us, lived two hundred yards away and were having a very noisy row.)* God willing, today is the climax and it is finished so I may contemplate all recent events.

Operation kept to. (I myself am over the hump – which one, though?)

28 July

Tonight the climax and the lesson learnt. It came about through the plea of the oration. Suddenly I understood – I, that which has descended into the Three worlds, pulling back up. (Yesterday evening I had decided to take off the brakes; if this was what I was supposed to be doing, then do it totally. In the daytime, today, total split disorientation.) I now must push push push from:

to:

With this Initiation, I now know what I am doing. Even the lower triangle has agreed that it is time to 'help' – we are working out our relationship. In the Oratory, it was clear Samadhi during which I was able to understand and see all this. Nothing can stop me now – nothing, for I know where I belong. If He designs to will it. The God Our Lord is all-powerful and it is only by His Mercy and Grace that I am at all, let alone have arrived here. He has only to look away and our Cosmos would die. What use then has He for us Initiates and Co.? None, except within the terms of His purpose which none of us can ever approach and understand. We exist – all Hierarchy, everything – by His Kind Grace and amazing tolerance.

Today I am much graced in His Love. May it flow to All and One in everything unto His Glory. Everything is adoration unto Him. Now must I burn through, if He so deigns to accept this wormly sacrifice. Truly. In this Universe I am nothing and this feeling transmutes itself to this early life – perhaps I am and know nothing at all and it is all delusion. No matter, as long as I may not be separate. He is the ocean and if we may be drops to fall into it, we are much honoured.

Operation kept to.

29 July

I do not really want to write this as I am not at all certain what is happening. All day I have been all right, knowing that I must remain quiet and look ever up (thanks to the *I Ching*), which was/ is truly the answer. This evening in the Oratory, things and feelings that I do not understand, energies that continue now. I am merging with I perhaps? *(The 'I' of my personality with the 'I' of my soul.)* I don't know and words heard that could only be incorrect – if so, whence did they come? Christ's name. (Diary stops as a toad walks in through the door.) (We *were often visited by toads from the river, but this was the only time that one actually hopped through the door.)* The toad freaked me. Good Heavens, what is happening? Obviously it is best to write no more until I understand. My faith in His mercy, though a slight feeling that I trust nothing, nothing at all. At this point? Obviously it is best...

Operation kept to.

(One hour later) The outcome of all the above being that I was allowed to appear to Frances. Was I? Will she retain the vision? *(By these kinds of statements I meant that I thought Frances could perceive me in my full spiritual potential.)* And me? What am I actually doing? *(During this whole period I was overwhelmed by my inner duality. I moved between two experiences of consciousness. In one, I am transpersonal, completely aware and present. In the other, I am fully identified with my thoughts and my personality. As well as being two different states of consciousness, they are also two completely different energy experiences. The difference between them was extreme and I was grappling to find the techniques and wilfulness to hold me in my transpersonal state.)*

30 July

The whole of the preceding tortuous period is over and *I* have emerged. Funnily in the Tibetan's *Esoteric Astrology* he refers to this as one of the tests through Scorpio: '...re-orients himself to the Monad and passes through most subtle tests to certain indefinable and spiritual recognitions'. Though ever a sinful worm before Our Lord, I dare now to know who I am and I dare to say that the worst is over. Now to hold my eyes ever upwards until the time comes. After that, I can have no concept. As always, new things being learned, new visions of living and His grandeur. New orientation and adjustment needed. Truly more praise unto Him than is possible – I have had to separate myself from my wife because of our behaviour and will remain so, I think, until after the Operation. *(Frances and I began to sleep in separate rooms.)* (I should have mentioned about five weeks ago that I stopped saying the Lord's Prayer, as I had enough on my plate.)

No matter how far we reach, always always we aspire higher. This is the Law. I must learn.

Operation kept to.

31 July
Despite all that has passed, it does not get any easier. Another round of battle begins – again, one in which I do not understand what is happening. Also, unimportant, I have a bad ulcer on the left side of my mouth, twitch on left of nose and a few days ago had left eardrum trouble. Answer?? Too much studying of astrology with notes, sucking energy from Manasic Left Eye??? *(Over-activity of the left hemisphere of the brain.)*
   Operation kept to.

1 August
Great rushes of energy and otherness. Frequent physical cata-lepsy, especially across my forehead. I am not trying hard enough to hold my head clear in the light, but then again I don't really know what I am doing. Glee, then torture. The Master D.K.(?) appeared again to Frances and said that he is watching over us. I am more grateful than can be imagined. The current time is truly the most interesting ever; what one might call a completely new dimension in living. I am being more flip than I mean to be.
   Operation kept to.

2 August
A great, great deal is happening – from the sublime to the ridicu-lous and back again. Firstly, a most amazing amount of energy is pouring through me which I can approximate to the 'rush' that heralds an LSD trip, but that has continued now for some days. Secondly, Frances continued her misbehaviour today and I virtu-ally beat her up which, to be exact, finally seems to have done the trick. *(I need to clarify what happened here. At the time Frances and I were surrounded and totally disorientated by the force of energy around us. This was a very real and tangible energy field. Anyone else who came near us physically would immediately begin to sweat. Neither Frances nor I showed our fear, but occasionally slipped into hysterical screaming at each other. On this occasion we actually got into a physical struggle and at one point I threw her from me on to the floor. We looked at each other in that strange atmosphere and suddenly entered a state of complete detachment from everything that was happening. It was a moment of pure zen satori, of reality suddenly becoming clear. We paused and noticed it. Frances found the moment extraordinary and interesting, and forgave the violence. In many ways our fight was simply an easing of tension. These many years later, however, I am still embarrassed by my*

pomposity and self-righteous attitude to her portrayed in the diary.) I also have learnt much from the episode. Thirdly, I am being persuaded that exteriorisation *(taking my consciousness consciously out of my body)* is now an important thing to do. Fourthly, the left-hand side of my face is in a mess, and a stomach-ache and many mosquito bites. I realised what I had to do this afternoon and actually drew this on my arm:

This worked. Then in the Oratory this evening – the only place where everything is normal – the same thing that occurred to me at the beginning of the Operation (when I was 'glowing' in my vainglorious innocence) struck me: that I must make all these sensations absolutely normal in my life and continue onwards. At the moment that almost elicits an hysterical giggle. No – I joke. Anyway and so – sinning ever more terribly in my weakness, my vanity and my fears – I continue.

Operation kept to.

3 August

From ecstasy to the verge of the traumatic and hysterical paranoia and lunacy and then back again. It is not possible to put all this in to words which would be directly understandable or useful. Extremes. Extremes of joy and bliss, and also extremes of fear, of standing alone shrieking on the edge of space through which one will float into infinity, tortured by every conceivable reality. Truly extremes – but *always* here. *This* must be the 'dark night of the soul' (though – joke – one seems to go through it every few months or so). Then this evening, a vision of strength as His servant – as must one of His Angels be – so His Son must stand strong and calm, praying only and directly to Him, while within one screams and twists but is held claustrophobically down. But He sees all and in that is the only strength and solution. I am one moment cocky still, the next a worm ever sinning, not knowing what to do, finding no advice I can understand (I do not comprehend the *Ching* any more or perhaps I do not want to). I know nothing and understand nothing about how I am being needfully thrown and tossed about like a puppet, as I watch approvingly (?) I'm still here, though – is that a problem?

Operation kept to.

(*3 August continued*) I have just re-read what I threw on the *Ching* and perhaps – perhaps only – I insult both it and myself. I put forward this picture of an hysteric being buffeted and tossed as he – I – stumbles along the Path – and this *is* true – BUT, I do so by my own choice and by my own actions, and I dare to say that despite my sins and wormhood, I progress every day in vision, understanding and my ability to serve. Certainly, day by day, I become more of a worm before Him, but it is I who am so learning and willing it. And I am less of... than before perhaps. *He* needs me not, though, and I exist, as do we all, by His grace and tolerance, and it is by that grace that I may be allowed to raise myself. With thanks.

I have a previously unexperienced pain in the head, but over the last few days there have been many previously unexperienced happenings. Again, Operation kept to. (Frances initiated finally.) (*I suddenly perceived Frances to be behaving in a completely new and loving way – or, at least, one that suited me!*)

4 August
Until this period is over I hardly think it worthwhile to try and describe what is occurring (but it is similar to yesterday), as I am not at all certain. Re-reading this diary, it seems as though it hasn't stopped for a good four months. All praise to Him.

Operation kept to.

5 August
Similar to yesterday. Yet again, my relationship with Frances is a problem. Why do we shame ourselves so? (What sort of play is it?) I think, however, that I *might* be emerging. If I ever do, I shall try to explain.

Operation kept to.

6 August
The energy continues – but now *Bliss*. As ever, I am watching to be certain. When I am, I shall write it in here. But I received from the

I Ching Hexagram 1, 'The Creative' with the fifth line changing, which I have long dreamed of. And before Him, I am still the greatest worm. I must relate upwards and exteriorise. *(It is worth quoting a few phrases from that first hexagram which is titled The Creative: 'The creative works sublime success... The movement of heaven is full of power. Thus the superior man makes himself strong and untiring.' Then the fifth changing line says: 'Flying dragon in the heavens. It furthers one to see the great man.')*
Operation kept to.

7 August

I think that I may now dare to write 'sensibly' about the last week or, to be more exact, the last period. It is impossible for me to pinpoint quite when it began; not to be flip, but only semi-serious, one might say at the age of seven/eight. At any rate the 'super-surge of white-light' energy began seven days ago to create its effects for this Initiation. I am not certain whether that energy belongs purely to the Initiation or whether it is under my domin-ion permanently. I do not wish in any way to lose it. It is most glorious and beautiful, and impossible to describe except by sensation – though anyone who has experienced LSD and been through what is called 'the white light high' might understand.

Anyway, now as always a time of readjustment and learning and assessing. On 24 July I wrote that I was there:

I now occupy the upper triangle and my time is spent in gently shushing the lower triangle until it is quietened completely. I am being as careful as I can be. Over the last six days I was not ever capable of reading (well, only two-thirds of Dante's *Inferno*!) and it was truly a most uncontrollable experience but with great heights of bizarre ecstasy about which I must no longer be so innocent. It is beautiful how these cycles of learning approximate exactly at each higher turn of the spiral.

At the end of the oration this evening, a 'heavy' of sorts visited, showing that I must surely return to normal capacity for cool behaviour (*with* the energy now passing through me). As the *I Ching* so succinctly put it after yesterday: Hexagram 23 'Splitting Apart' with the first five lines changing!
The Operation as a whole now makes perfect sense and I feel 'righteous' in demanding the favour and Grace that I ask of Him,

though I be ever a worm. I shall not push exteriorising as the correct time will be when it happens for a truly useful purpose, which I imagine to be after Initiation Five or Liberation when one must be led, the humble aspirant, to the White Lodge at Sirius, as described by the Master D.K. Again, I feel nervous every time I dare to *actually* think or state where I may be now, but I am a White Magician and I have now appeared – though I am ever a wormlike aspirant that is allowed to exist by His loving, kindness and tolerance.

Operation kept to.

8 August

Last night, before or as I dropped off to sleep, a great sucking blast of white light that quite frightened me; and I turned away from it like a paranoid dog which will not look into a well-meaning man's eyes. Then, this morning, intense sacral activity which I did not control. Then I read a passage by the Master D.K. about whether the aspirant is strong enough to continue; also the *I Ching* said, irreparable damage. So I have started putting the whip heavily across myself again. 'I' must take *no* notice of the lower triangle in the:

which in my weakness I watch and take great and 'silly' notice of; similarly this lower triangle must truly become a *loving* and perfect reflection of the upper so that there is no friction. I have seen also extremely clearly a bizarre and horrible vanity and arrogance in myself which has and is shaming me most terribly before Him. Though what I now say might also be vanity, I feel that I can get over and through it. I am truly trying as desperately (almost) as I can. The real point is that I must keep my Taurian (*I am in fact an Aquarian*) focus ever up unto Him; this, the case, I *cannot* sin. But at this moment I am too pathetically weak and feeble and sometimes scared to look up all the time and *not* to hear that voice below that squeaks up at me. That voice must be made 'loving and lovable' as well. I spend some time experimenting with exteriorization – unsuccessfully – which is not very important, as I see how easy it will be at Liberation. I must learn and correct myself carefully. But the incredible bliss of His love!

Operation kept to.

9 August

Again, last night three to four hours of blasting energy, which I do not understand properly. The day a strain as I truly see the separateness of the lower triangle and my attention focused on it. The disorientation is occasionally leading to paranoia – about which I am learning. I would like to be through this period. Three words keep echoing through me: III, Saturn and Christ.

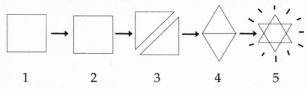

I seem to be always slipping from (5) to (3). I am finding it all quite hard at the moment – but deservedly so if I am to progress (that is the first time that I have ever written that unhappily).

Operation kept to.

10 August

It is difficult to write anything. The process continues, but the energies and the concepts are very subtle, elating or nerve-racking. At times I feel vibrantly strong and warrior-like – physically able to live a good semi-millennium. The Tibetan's books are, naturally, without equal as they are the Hierarchy's Teachings and of great import to me. *(Hierarchy in this context is a word sometimes used to describe the inner invisible world of perfected humans and liberated beings.)* They are educating me. Yesterday I understood the *true* mystery of sex and how strange that I should have missed the point for so long. (Joke: A master is in a perpetual state of Big O – is that too vulgar? Forgive me.) But that, I think, is the truth of raising the *kundalini* energy from the base of the spine to the head centre. I may be doing that anyway for at the moment my main preoccupation is with grabbing rampant personality traits or emotions and transmuting them immediately into spiritual energy. The slightest trait must be caught and changed. This is the true point, is it not? To be liberated, one must be the Perfect Man. One is not *yet* the Perfect Man. God willing, one may all be.

Operation kept to.

(Five minutes later) In Oratory tonight, at a point of intense concentration and transmutation which centred in forehead, felt minor electric shock. Whether it was hostile, benevolent or self-

induced (as I had five minutes earlier had a 'naughty' thought about someone disturbing my prayer – which was *why* I was in intense state) I do not know – but it made me react in strength as though bitten by a gnat. I know nothing, as ever, and my behaviour shames me.

11 August

A new feeling, understanding, vision. Firstly His Will (as always courtesy of the Tibetan's Teachings). Secondly, myself: a severe case of amnesia out of which I am slowly waking. Who? I know not, but Will, Wise-Love, Intelligence is the essence, interfered with by the personality that I have picked up since I lost my memory (how many years? 43 or 777?), though I enjoy its humour. What to do except watch and wait? If I could remember and know who I truly am and what I am supposed to be doing, then there would be nothing to write. But I am not perfect, am I? And that must be the nub of the matter. I know nothing about all this yet, but I think/feel almost. Many times now I am I until me interferes and I am too weak to avoid it/me. A duo, a bodyguard of 'nasties' in Oratory this evening: I am, by His Grace, rising above them. A continuation, in fact, of extremes that lead ever closer to fusion, from shame to wisdom, from weakness to will. By His Grace.

Operation kept to.

12 August

Strange – all day I felt as though, in a way, I was taking a holiday. No great strain or energies. Occasional questioning of identity and identifying with that newness. Then, this evening, the whole valley is grey and I feel most heavily threatened – threatened, not frightened. (The truth being, though I have hardly dared write it earlier, that the weather in the valley is totally related to 'me' or vice versa – to, I suppose, a most startling degree which 'I' have taken casually.) What concerns me most about this threat is that it interferes with my orison, as I am aware of It and, during the orison, my total and complete vision should be nothing but upward – which shows that I sin in daring to fear this Mayan *(illusory)* threat more than I fear the reality of His Glory. At the moment I am living inside this threat and can do nothing but wait. I feel quite calm and nicely resigned to anything, feeling calm in my awareness of tension and that perhaps I can rise above *any* threat...Then again, 'I' may be moving backwards, slipping into

the warm dung and not knowing it. Whichever, I sin feebly before
Him and am weak and pathetic and cocky in my shame for all that.
I am re-reading *Cosmic Fire* of which I am now understanding 80
per cent(?).
    Operation kept to.

13 August
Almost forgot to write tonight. Last night's threat disappeared this
morning and I put the whip across my back again (semi-continuous concentration/meditation, semi-fasting) with immediate effects: rush of energy and two searing moments of duality which
approached total paranoid hysteria, but all over and calm now. I
think this afternoon I was in semi-exteriorized meditation. I was
'greeted' by two sheaves of silver light – I am not sure. But to be
certain: although I learn ever more about my true vanity, weakness and sinfulness, yet I feel there is some progress being made;
but that, too, is vanity. I am a bad behaver yet.
    Operation kept to.

14 August
Progress, perhaps, and sinfulness. A story (funny perhaps, shaming certainly): a letter that I wrote today stuck vainly and separately in my mind and, during the orison this evening, I ended my
appeal to the Angels: 'Yours sincerely, Amen.' Oi. Shame and, in
fact, some confusion.
    Operation kept to.

15 August
Backwards and forwards; wormhood, weakness and sins. But I
think that perhaps I may have a vision in my meditation of spirit
being my essence which may rule the day. It strikes me that I
should note that my daily regimen is one-and-a-half hours prayer,
one hour meditation, five hours of holy reading and messing
about. I *am* trying and I think that in my dreams I have visited the
outside corridors of the Academy.
    Operation kept to.

16 August
Progress that I find impossible to quite write about. The Tibetan
has said it all. A calm, then a shame. Holding the whip tight. A
difficult balance between humility and elation, almost. Much

much shame. Heavy attack last night (in bed) and in the Oratory yesterday and today – the heaviest yet, but coped with. A burning warm sensation at the back of my neck.

Operation kept to.

17 August

The fact that it is now only five weeks to the End somewhat boggles but hardly surprises me. Some progress. Greater understanding always of my sinfulness. Instructions continually on how to behave. I am trying. As always, I am a worm and do not dare to know anything. 'Heavies' again in the Oratory; I think the theory is to gradually build them up – if I can pray with them threatening me, then I shall not be terrified on the day. I do not know anything for certain except that: if nothing happens, if the rest of this life is spent anywhere, I am grateful for having been allowed to pray to Him in His beauty for Six Months. Everything is vanity and I count myself, though a worm and sinner, Blessed by His grace.

Operation kept to.

18 August

Increasing awareness – which highlights my sins and weaknesses. Up and down. A very useful *mantram* suddenly in use at the moment: Be Here Now. I am here now for a period; then I'm where? when? and back again. New visions, certainly, but of nothing am I certain. How can I be certain of anything while everything that was me – my personality – still acts, rearing its ugly head. To be perfect with all that, God willing. I am such a cocky little worm. (Burning at back of neck continues.)

Operation kept to.

19 August

An attack first thing this morning; another as I write this. In the daytime much energy and light flowing through me. It is a very intense and strange time. My head also aches, throbs, pressures. In the Oratory this evening, a 'high' that I do not understand at all. Another voice? Perhaps my personality playing very devious tricks? All most peculiar, and as I write this, quite heavy. I really don't quite understand. I am, I must admit, fearful. I put my faith in our Lord and His protection, but even so I am beginning to find it a bit heavy still to be objectively completely on my own through this. The Master D.K. mentioned somewhere about some Initiates becoming involved in planetary *karma* – I don't know. I do know, however, that I *am* moving and *must* stay in/with it whatever of the Three Worlds tries to threaten and suck me back.

Operation kept to.

20 August

Moments of great certainty alternating with weak fear and separateness. Strength and quiet *versus* cocky whininess. The orison now very intense. I cannot write a full description for fear this diary falls into the wrong hands, because it has to do with raising the *kundalini* fire – I think. I am not certain, but I trust to intuition. More attacks last night, finally pushing me into trying to state with belief that I exist in consciousness on the Buddhic *(the plane of pure intuitive consciousness)* plane and that no threat from the Three Worlds could touch me – but it does touch my personality. No? My personality plays more and more devious games in order to stay around; I am continually astonished by its/my ability to surface into control – this is my true weakness and sin as my personality is bizarrely cocky and needs slapping down (though with love??).

Operation kept to.

21 August

The beginning of the last month. I am beginning – but only just – to be my true self. That which I was I still am; it irritates me greatly, is occasionally strong – that is, in relation to my weakness – and I sin most terribly in allowing my eyes to look down and take notice. With no other objective advice, the I Ching is my most amazing and truthful friend. I cannot thank His Wisdom sufficiently in helping me. It is bizarre which parts of me exist still there – from an extremely vain bourgeois to a paranoid hysteric as regards the course and outcome of this Operation.

I am struck by my strange and terrible 'jumping-the-gun' in the past, even now, and fear whether it will be held against me. Even now I dare to think it shall not. For the first time I *(the transpersonal, soul-identified 'I')* am writing this diary – three inches back from my eyes; I intend to stay here. I intend to be strong and hold in the light. Even though I am I, I know nothing of the present or the future. I am a most lucky worm and my trust is in the Hierarchy as They work out His Plan. I pray only that I be allowed to help – that They deign to allow me to wipe Their feet. That I might, in no matter what way, be a part of Their Work. If, even now, I am worthy. Truly, I know nothing. In Christ.

Operation kept to.

22 August

I am writing this diary again. I have been around for quite a lot of the day – though not enough. I am now the upper triangle looking down at my lower, trying not to be distracted, trying to notice *when* I am distracted and continue to sin. The level of consciousness is Buddhic *(mainly intuitive)*, but I do not hold it. My thoughts, my meditation are in words, in clothed mental matter. I must learn two things: (*a*) to hold steady in the light; (*b*) to meditate Buddhically. It could, therefore, I muse, be an extremely long time until the next step is taken. My personality either mopes and obstructs or else is a Master fixing up the World already. I am, when I am not separate, not sinning, without time, in bliss, and faced with a vista that shows I am merely a worm poking my head out of the dung and occasionally – no frequently – slipping back in. All praise, all glory, all service to the One God, Our God by whose Grace and Loving kindness we are.

Operation kept to.

23 August

'I' am here – with difficulty, however, always sinning, always pathetically and weakly looking down. I am, I consider often, a spiritual cripple of rare standing, looking continually for occult boosts to keep me chugging happily along. I want out.

Etheric vision and clairvoyance commencing, flashing in and out as I try and intuit the yoga to bring it together. D.K.'s *Cosmic Fire* creates ideas and concepts far too large for me. I think I have been extremely vain – I know nothing. I still experience much fear at times; a note in *Cosmic Fire* says fear is due to the reactions of the *devas* that make up the etheric body; I hope so and I think anyway that I have had a sufficiency. A thunderstorm today and I dare to imagine that the times of real pain and torture are over. I cannot keep my vision upwards – I am a truly sinful worm – and I am worried: twenty-nine days is not very long, but God is my shield if and as He deigns to notice.

Operation kept to.

24 August

Just – but only just – a little bit less naughty today. The vision mainly centred upwards. The problem at this moment is with the lives of which my body is made up – Devas VIII, VI, V (*I am referring here to the living essence that makes up the matter of my physical, emotional and mental body)* – who are responding to all vibrations around me in a different way from my consciousness. It would seem that the issue now is for my consciousness to stay steady, while the rest of me comes fully under the laws of Vishnu or Love at which point they will have been raised to the required state for the next planetary round. (Whoever reads this will have to have the Tibetan's terms of reference – which are the Hierarchy's.) Perhaps if I had a *mantram* it would help. I do not know. If I am being wrong about all this, then I sin in a *most* horrible and disgusting way. *But* I am ever a worm.

The swifts and swallows are now flying within several (six-nine) feet of me. Each day also seems to have a regular cycle: I pray and then go back to bed, always heavily centring myself first; when I get up the second time I am immersed in *(psychological)* concrete and some unpleasantness but not much. Then things get progressively better, climaxing at about 4 pm and then get progressively worse, climaxing again about 6.30 pm *(I am referring to bad moods and bad atmospheres.)* Before I go to bed, I usually experience some fear. It has been like this every day for about a week now. In the early hours of the night, though, I am introduced to flashes of love and consciousness that are beyond words; last night was truly indescribable. I *think* I have completely raised the *kundalini* fire. I am here and then I am not. Let me hold still and not sin.

Operation kept to.

25 August

Still a bit better, but only a bit. Have finished re-reading *Cosmic Fire*; the concepts dazzle me. I am now reading D.K.'s (oh, much love and gratitude to Him) *Rays and Initiations*. He suggests the 'three demands' that will 'make' the final jump. I do not understand. I sin still.

Operation kept to.

26 August

Without the Tibetan's writings, I would be completely lost. As it is, I am just lost. Also, in orisons, information slips through to me about what is happening and what I should do, but I fear always that I am sinning by 'looking away' from Him to whom I confess. I believe the situation is this (if I am wrong, I sin in most terrible vanity): 'I' am Spirit and Matter; I cannot equate the two; the matter is not fully shining yet; the physical shall be golden, the emotional shall be Buddhic loving; and the mental, pure spiritual will (I think). But All This must become One as it is all life within life – and I am, therefore, lost. The physical sensations are most strange, but I have been here most of today except for about an hour. Truly I am not at all certain of anything. I know nothing about the present or the future; even the past only now becomes slightly clear. I keep being instructed to bring people into the group; one more today. It now amounts to around twelve. B.P.(!); A.A.; M.J.; G.H.F.; J.K.; M.D.A.; M.H.; S.I.; G.A.; S.B.; R.J.; F.J.(?); H.C.A. *(These are all initials of friends whom I held in my prayers and meditations.)* I am certain of none of them in reality; four are very close; perhaps I am being unjust? And WHO is certain of me? Anyone?

Operation kept to.

27 August

The writings of the Tibetan are completely reorientating me. One of the 'problems' has been that I have had no conscious contact with the Hierarchy and have therefore been able to rely on nothing except my faith in His Glory and Grace ('nothing except'?!!). The Operation is a magic one to gain dominion over 'spirits and all creatures' – but, in fact, it has been the burning ground of initiation. And now, today, I find myself an initiate, still with no Hierarchical Contact (consciously). *(The next day I wrote in the diary "Full Moon in May, idiot!" This referred to the 17th May when I had full communication with my Master. In the first published edition of this diary I wrote in at this point this footnote: "This is a neat example of the dichotomy that can exist in a human mind between the word-based mental and the higher intuitive faculties. Despite all the clear guidance that I had received, at that point in time I still frequently hedged my bets on the reality of telepathic communication. A registered letter would have suited me better." I also ignored the physical manifestation of the Tibetan teacher.)*

I begin to sense and feel concepts and glories that the Tibetan can also only hint at in words in his books and I see also, through his teaching, the most beautiful picture of the forward movement not only of humanity, but of everything that is within the sphere of our planetary Logos. *(The soul or inner consciousness of the whole planet.)* Yet, am I still overwhelmed with my wormhood and sinfulness, my – to put it in more modern terms and out of the

Bible-belt mystic jargon – inadequacy to serve in any way, my presumption in even daring to attempt to be allowed in, my impatience to move forward, and still my fear. But I now see a way forward; the dark of which I have been afraid is the pureness of spirit. I am spirit and matter, and cannot see the unity within myself. My personality truly 'irritates me', to quote the Master D.K. I am speeding. I do not seem able to hold my head correctly, my eyes focused, and when I do, the pressure, *in fact*, on my skull is bizarre and painful.

If I am IV *(I am referring again to an initiatory level)* then I must, I imagine, behave in a certain correct manner – so must I do. There is no more to be said or whined about. What the end of the Operation holds, however, is altogether another matter, with its wands and robes. 'I' have not written all this. Duality, I seek to show the reader/myself, is still rampant but observed. I wish love and strength to all who follow. By His Grace and unto His glory.

Operation kept to.

28 August

Last night, the pressure on my skull increased and a flow of incredible energy went through me which I directed out to the *Ashram. (By 'Ashram' I meant the group of friends, known and unknown, with whom I felt myself to be linked.)* I do not know if this was correct. What I must now do is hold my consciousness ever at the Buddhic level, ever in the space where thought is *not* expressed in words. I hold it: then I lose it. When I hold it, through it I see a great glory. I am boggled by the fact that I have seen His Eye. *(One of my experiences during these days was as if I were fully in the presence of Divinity, face to face, looking directly into God's eyes. Earlier in the diary I remark that I was like a frightened dog looking into the eyes of its master. Of everything that happened during the Operation, that particular experience was perhaps the most important. It is an experience which has never left me, in which I am still living and to which I am still adjusting. I no longer find the light blinding or humbling, but I am still in awe of it.)* I now will to move steadily ahead – despite my spiritual presumptuousness, my continual 'lowering of the vision' – by His Grace and unto His Glory.

Operation kept to.

29 August

A day in which a certain clarity is emerging. Firstly, page 517 of

Rays and Initiations perfectly describes the problem, but I am commencing feebly to sound the *mantram* of 'Purpose itself I am', presupposing that I am a Third Ray initiate. *(This section from Rays and Initiations reads: " It is not easy for the disciple on this ray to achieve the necessary focal point of silence; his intense fluidity leads to many words or to great mental activity, frequently carried forward under the impulse of glamour. This lessens the potency of what he seeks to do. But when he has succeeded in achieving 'mental silence' and is simply a point of intelligent concentration, then he can use the Word of Power (the inner note of his own spirit) with great effectiveness. The difficulty is that he has to overcome the tendency to use it with the idea of physical plane results in his consciousness. Always he works from the angle of that divine quality which characterises matter... But once he intuitively comprehends and factually grasps the concept that spirit-matter are one reality, and once he has achieved within himself the sublimation of matter, then he can divorce himself from all that the human being understands in relation to form.)* Still, vast amounts of energy are flowing through me and I am learning to control it, and hold myself steady. It is having a very extreme physical effect in terms of ear- and head-ache on those around me, and any non-initiate has difficulty within some twenty feet of my presence. I have been given a big magical act to do which will, I think, culminate during October – I am not certain, as I have not properly meditated on the act to create a pure 'soul for the form'. *(I thought that I was involved in meditational and energy work to help transform the ongoing Middle Eastern crisis.)*

I *am* being trained and I am moving ahead. Though I am ever a total worm before Him, before All, before the One. The world news today was also encouraging!!! But I am still spiritually presumptuous.

Operation kept to.

30 August

A very unhappy day. A concerted effort, starting last night in my sleep with sexual desire, and continuing right through the day to disrupt my centredness – and successfully disrupting it 90 per cent of the time. A bad ulcer in the left-hand side of my face; and the similarities to 31 July are very interesting. I have finished *Rays and Initiations* and I need to slow my mind down to a controllable snail's pace, to have control *every second* of the mental forms emanating from me. Apart from the fact that I *must* do this for my own progress, they are extremely potent and therefore 'unpleasantly' interferesome to others. I must hold myself still, knowing who I am and what I must do. Really, today has made me unhappy and has been somewhat tortuous, but I think I know what I must do in terms of vision and work. No doubt, I will ask the beloved *Ching* if I am missing anything.* I am somewhat disgusted with myself, yet I have been shown how I must be. Though I had the feeling at one point that I had been deliberately thrown back to teach me. A most severe attack in the Oratory this evening. Yet I live! I also sin still.

    Operation kept to.

* Yes, it tells me I am missing being 'joyous' (Hexagram 58).

31 August

Three weeks to go! I am, I think, looking forward to it. I have been on edge today – no reading at all, mainly a semi-continuous meditation. I feel that I am on the edge of understanding the mystery of spirit-matter and 'the purpose itself I am'. And I ever repeat to myself the Master D.K.'s words that the physical dense body is not a principle. Therefore I need not even think about it. My personality irritates me truly. I must be truly free of all form, but I am not. I remain, for instance, interested in my – who? – financial future. Whether or not I emerge from all this, money is *not* relevant. I bullshit that if I am to be useful, I must be free. I am not concerned or obsessed; I am casually interested and that is too much, too interferesome. Generally I have not been very good today. As I commence slightly to understand things, I become impatient for results, ever forgetting that results only come from going more carefully and beautifully. The business of holding the mental energy under control is very useful. I begin to plead correctly for conversation with His Angels.

    Operation, by His Grace, kept to.

1 September

I am learning now all the time: how to control, how to 'orchestrate' myself and my effect on others. I am seeing more and, therefore, becoming increasingly aware of my deficiencies. *But* I think that it is all clear; the issues are obvious and I dare to think that the pain of my own *karma* is over. If I am wrong, Lord be merciful and kind with me. Also I feel that it is only now that I am beginning to pray correctly, to 'influence' myself properly, to invoke successfully, to plead with the most minuscule justification. The main fight is with a mind that races and continually jumps the gun, that fights in an opposite, though not wicked, direction from slowing, loving, intuitive watchfulness. I am still prepared, however, for some heavy surprises – which will, of course, be deserved as I still, in shame, sense a disgusting vanity. I do not know. All Glory to the One.

Operation kept to.

2 September

The 'heavy surprise' did come last night. Blasts of energy and information; a vision of something unpleasant – all continuing until I was too exhausted to be able to take any more. I am/was ashamed by my nervousness at one point and the fact that I did not dive into it. I have not behaved as correctly as I should have done today. Am now reading *Esoteric Psychology* – the Master D.K. has much (page 122) to say about Devas that make this 'medieval' (though Blessed be Abra-Melin and Abraham) Operation. The *kundalini* fire is being raised even higher. My etheric body is wobbling somewhat. The pain of the intense pressure on the inside cavities of my skull has subsided somewhat now; though the shape of the physical head has changed somewhat. I am enjoying what is happening now. I don't really know what I'm doing or how things will proceed, but I am in good and loving hands though I sin and shame myself.

Operation kept to.

3 September

The energy today 'running against' me (and the rest of the world?) and I had great difficulty in 'stancing' correctly, though the *Ching* suggested that Grace was appropriate. What is strange and on my mind is a feeling that the suffering and pain is more or less over. The Path which has led to this meagre point of aspiration has ever been one of psychic pain and, although I look and scream for a release into that bliss, the idea of that pain truly ending is not something that I can easily accept. It shames me. Added to my wormhood I truly feel shamed. I think of my wandering mind, my spiritual presumptuousness, my total ignorance and separateness, and then I think to the Master Jesus and, today, to Solzhenitsyn – and I feel more shame. And the Christ who descended to raise us all. What have I done to merit any release, other than aspire to something which it is a vanity for me to even think of? And this shame mixed today with some impatience, impatience that these weeks be over, that I can stop putting out all my aspirational energies purely for a successful ending to this Operation, that He may deign to allow me to serve in conscious knowledge of what I truly do. Yes, I am sending energies and thoughts, and making White Magic as much as I can, but I do not really know what is happening. There! We have the double-bind. What vanity to think that I am evolved enough to be allowed to know *consciously* how I am serving. I am distributing good energy and thoughtforms through this planet in a time of great upheaval – and is it not enough that I know that? There are enough people doing good with no knowledge at all, but purely for love. All very introverted, no? Grace and joy unto His service – a sufficiency. May He forgive me.

Operation kept to.

4 September

Very similar feelings to yesterday, all somewhat heightened by an extremely loose etheric body which, during this evening's oration, somewhat unnerved me. The *Ching* 'accuses' me of 'modesty about being modest' (or tells me that is what I should be – that sounds a bit coy, but I am still too nervous to take any chances). Again, voices and sensations that I do not quite understand. One part of me says I should not exteriorize until I am taken by the hand by friends and know where I am going; the other opinion is that I am going to exteriorize whether I like it or not, and that I do have the 'right' to behave like one of Dante's imperious Angels. Mmm. Also, yesterday and today with my own eyes I have seen the reality of the back-to-front nature of the Astral – at least some other dimension – which is the ultimate fantasy and *maya* for humanity. (Thus Hitler's inverted globe and Carroll's *Alice Through the Looking Glass*.) *(For a while, looking out across the valley, I entered an altered state of consciousness. Everything dissolved into a blur of crystals and sparks, and then reappeared – except that it was all inside out as if looking into a distorting mirror, with the furthest away closest and so on.)*

The most beautiful aspect of the moment, though, is that all that has happened is that I see a beginning, that I now see the door which heralds real life. A casual reader may wonder at the fact that I am unimpressed by the relative elevation of my consciousness – but this is only in emotional/personality human terms. And it is only now that I begin to see the true wonder and harmony of this planet, let alone system or universe. The depths of my ignorance are really quite unfathomable. I write too much. I burble on. It is a form of childish excitement still tinged with nervousness. I am, however, learning Psalm XIC off by heart – and that *is* my protection as it has ever been. That the Earth should be One in Love by all its brethren. Again, however, the same shame as yesterday.

Operation kept to.

(Psalm 91 begins: He that dwelleth in the secret place of the Most High shall abide under the shadow of the Almighty. It also contains the line: For he shall give his Angels charge over thee, to keep thee in all thy ways. And ends: With long life will I satisfy him, and shew him my salvation.)

5 September

Much happening. My etheric body wobbling greatly unless I am consciously with my dense body when I move, though in prayer I keep feeling that I am going to topple over. Great pressure inside my head; also, interestingly, if I push my finger against a certain point on my skull – where hair changes direction – pressure is felt over the forehead. What? I do not know. Then a great illumination this evening that everything that exists of my threefold personality should be below my threshold of consciousness but readily retrievable when needed; sit back and watch it function, for instance, in certain social situations while I carry on with my work, is the correct aim if in a 'social' situation by mistake. I am learning. Changes and awarenesses are happening rapidly, but a feeling of imminent calm and bliss that will be total. I am 'nervous' at this moment of writing because I think something may occur tonight. Funnily, the fight is to always retain total and complete awareness – even now – the bothering thing is mainly that it continually feels as though my etheric body will take off without my *conscious* decision. Considering everything, that is hardly a real problem. I am rambling, as has my mind for much of today. A reader who wishes to know everything should read the works of the Tibetan. And still some shame.

Operation kept to.

Almost forgot. An interesting double-bind is that all the magical acts that can be used if this Operation is successful are very 'personal' and separate, i.e., Conflict. This arises as I prepare for the conjurations.

6 September

Similar feelings to the last two days. A climax, though, in terms of
no more whining about my sinfulness before God. Again the *Ching*
directed me, released the intuition. I must no longer suck 'nourish-
ment' of those above me; it is now my task to nourish myself and
others. In prayer, "I stand high above the eighteen fires and sound
out my demands.' There is no other language that is suitable. As
I was re-preparing the magic squares and re-reading what I must
do over the seven days, I suddenly appreciate how I may truly
invoke these forces, and that I am vibrantly strong now – my own
magic circle; the one slight, and interesting trouble is that the
remnants of the mind of my personality tend to think over the
question of invocation which, with my current vibrance, is almost
sufficient to attract immediately the forces; I, therefore, keep
silence. I feel and I am strong now. God willing.

The swallows who have a nest on the house are teaching Junior
how to fly. Mmm. May we all so learn, eh.

To His Glory. By His Grace.

Operation kept to.

7 September

The pace continues and I am not holding myself as high as I ought.
I feel that I had a holiday most of today, spending too much time
watching the baby swallows, four in all, learn how to fly. They are
very sweet. Swallows, swifts, the trees at the bottom of the farm
and the french beans were my only friends when I truly needed
them! The pressure inside my head is bizarre, as though the whole
of my cranium is being inflated; if I press on any point of the skull,
I feel the pressure on the opposite side. So if I lie down with the
back of my head on a pillow, it feels as if the front of my face will
take off. I think this is all an adjustment so that I may still use this
body, yet be clairvoyant, clairaudient, etc., to the point needed. I
understand better today the three demands which I sound out
from above. They are in the prayer of the 'Great Invocation'.

Operation kept to. All Glory to the One.

*(The Great Invocation is a very powerful and useful prayer if one moves
beyond its slightly sexist and patriarchal language into its true cadence
and intention:*

From the point of Light within the mind of God
Let light stream forth into the minds of men
Let light descend on Earth.

From the point of Love within the heart of God
Let Love stream forth into the hearts of men
May Christ return to Earth.

From the centre where the Will of God is known
Let purpose guide the little wills of men
The purpose which the Masters know and serve.

From the centre which we call the race of men
Let the Plan of Love and Light work out
And may it seal the door where evil dwells.

Let Light and Love and Power restore the Plan on Earth.)

7 September (continued)

Thirty minutes later, 10 pm, a little baby swallow sitting alone on the window ledge. Now in a box in the house, snuggled in cotton-wool. Coincidence? Special fate? Or the outcome of my thoughtform – I hope not? *(This was a beautiful gift of nature. In the midst of all the psychic turmoil, one of the baby swallows could not make its way home. It sat on our window ledge and allowed me to pick it up and then place it safely in a little box. It was very calm and seemed very happy. For some reason I christened it 'Herbie-Baby.' It rejoined its family the next morning.)*

8 September

I am not at all happy with the quality of energy that I have been putting out today. I thought today of a way that I could really be useful to the Plan in relation to communications and media. Herbie-baby, the swallow, spent a quiet night and joined his family late this morning. Truly, I am not happy with today; to be more exact, my energies in reaction to it.

Operation kept to. At one point today I thought, if I am truly a high initiate, then the qualifications are not very stringent. Then again, to be flippant, if I am only a low initiate, then there are thousands, which *is* a cheering thought for all of us. All praise to the Lord.

Re. my wife: the mist in which I found myself is due to the fact that in addressing her (soul) I took *real* notice of her personality. That will never happen again – with anyone. (Autumn started two days ago.)

9 September

A heavy day. Hmm. The swallows leaving, autumn beginning, the stars surging, I suppose, add to it, but a feeling of deep, deep pain from somewhere so profound inside it swells up. A pain that I have known and felt since childhood, but which I have not felt for perhaps twelve months as it was made secondary to my personal torture. But it was – as I write this I remember – that infinite hurt and sadness that consciously started me along the way this lifetime. It is that same sadness, incorrectness of the present situation for man, that has, I believe, turned every disciple's face 'towards Jerusalem' (to go up to). Not for the individual – though we scream for peace and liberation – but for all of us. Free the Men! Free the Children! Free the Women! The Birds! The Statues! The Plants! And then us, we squeak, please dear God. And so we all move forward.

Today, in midday prayer, I hope that I took all the brothers and sisters in my group up a step. My head is intensely pressured. I raised the 'serpent power' higher, slightly unnerving myself. My etheric is wobbling a lot. In my oration this evening, I felt the whole of this solar system to be a vast gothic cathedral vault! or vice versa. Yes? Pain and Great Beauty. Father, come to us all.

Operation kept to.

10 September

I am most surprised to find myself writing this, but today has been rather heavy with all energies running against me. *I* am still here but I have descended into being able to clearly see 'me' – the 'descent into hell' after which I shall rise, or just bad energy? But *I* am not changed, which is why the episode surprises me. Other atmospheres and energies surrounding the orations. It will, God willing, happen. I feel the Angels close by. I feel Uriel. I am being educated in an attitude to the evil spirits. I theenk. Again, today is not at all good. Though I will/can not behave badly, there is an element to my consciousness today which is retrogressive.

Operation kept to.

11 September

The energies today have been disgusting and I have been allowing them to pass through me. I am descended into the shit and hell, and I have watched myself so descending. Ha. Ha. But I am here. Oh, the doubts and agonies that appear, the pain deep down, the

infinite feeling of personal shittyness that negates all my aspiration. I *am* being serious. It is at times very, very dark and in this
darkness I do not shine as a light; therefore, sinfulness and
weakness. The *Ching* says 'modesty' – I am modest or immodest?
I am not certain. It is important for any friend who reads this to
realise that even at this stage, there are the most heavy doubts; not
about any of the Truths or His Wonder and Unity – but about
oneself and one's continual weakness and sin. That the energy
today should be so warped and that I should sink with it... It is
today or tomorrow the full moon. As such I have been praying
with as great an intensity as possible for my brothers and sisters,
and for my group; to keep them up and pushing through this time.
It is obviously a period of great importance for the Hierarchy and
I try to intuit how I may help, other than turning myself, if He so
wills, into another beacon of light. Whatever, the Forces of Light
are winning and the total vision is very exciting. The Kingdom of
God is approaching.
Operation kept to.

12 September

Similar to yesterday, except worse. The duality is painful in its
irritation. I am, but I had not the strength or will to *be* all day, and
became lost in my own illusory daydreams. Then suddenly, 'me'
would groan from deep within to be and be unpleasantly or at least
in fantasy, and some pain as it was pushed back down. What galls
me is that I knew something like this, in terms of opposing energy,
would happen and I had wanted to stay up in order to truly help
the group; to shine as the sun at midday as the *I Ching*, dear friend,
told me this morning with Hexagram 1 'The Creative with the
second, fifth and sixth lines changing, the last line of which I do not
fully understand. (Also, Allende dead, twelve killed in South
Africa – the crisis stumbles on.) Yet, some great change is also
happening. Sometimes I am here above myself, almost true and
complete, and then I slip back. In a suit of light and glory, and then
I slip. Last night, again a dream involving the Academy, I think,
with the Menuisier leading prayers. *(By 'Academy' I mean the
spiritual school many of us remember attending while asleep. It is named
after Plato's Academy. The Menuisier was an aged Berber carpenter
whose image I projected in my dream on to the real teacher.)*I am not
happy with myself at all today. Twelve days of it now, starting
intensely five days ago. Enough.
Operation kept to.

13 September

Similar energies and reactions to those of yesterday; if anything, worse. It's a sort of 'suck'. Whatever, being permanently (or much of the time at any rate) in the planetary cathedral in the company of Angels as a mental stance has helped, even though I hardly merit the august environment and presences. Yet even so – and I am sticking my neck out – I feel that this period too may be coming to an end. My feelings about the end of this Operation are neutral. My trust is in God and the Hierarchy. I know more or less what I am doing, and *I* am not afraid (though the matter of my personality occasionally starts still and is frightened). Sometimes there is an extremely distant voice that almost inaudibly squeaks that this is not a real thing. I myself disagree with that opinion. As ever, it seems that I know absolutely nothing. I am submerged in the Three Worlds, yet this afternoon began a feeling of just a little bit of glee. I am holding it back. Initiation must take a second place (to be exact, my compulsively vain thoughts on Initiation) to the success of this Operation. My trust is in the loving hands of Those who deign to guide me through this, despite my continual wormhood and weakness.

14 September

However sane and strong I may sound or be as I write this, today has been a day of profound darkness and, at times, profound fear. The fear is that I will be the one and only accident ever – the one that they on t'other side got. *Not* possible. I know the Laws and it is not possible. God, His protection, even my own power. There was also an attack last night in which my dream-body was caught and claustrophobically held; it did not frighten me. But today, in the darkness, the small whelps of personality from deep within have echoed out to above and I have lost any form of continuous Buddhic consciousness. Aloree and however, from this I will shortly emerge. I am preparing heavily (!?) for the last seven days at the moment. There is something very hot (in temperature) at my left shoulder in the Oratory as I pray.

On a completely different tack, certain questions have been arising over such scientifica as Light, Electricity, Evolution. Mmm. I know absolutely nothing, nothing at all. I must focus continuously upwards and out of the darkness.

Operation kept to. Were it not for a remark by the Master D.K. concerning darkness and initiation, I *would* be very worried.

15 September

No sleep last night with the feeling all the time that I was about to get up, and I went out to pray before dawn, the earliest yet, which I shall continue to do until the end of the Operation. Well, the heaviest day yet. My mind slips from between my eyes down to my solar plexus, which is more sensitive than ever before. Deep and horrible darkness, and I hold the whip most strongly across my back to pull me up. For a moment this afternoon, I thought I was emerging, but an environmental intrusion created a reaction in my solar plexus and I shot down. For the first time ever, in my orations this afternoon and evening, I *begged* to be released. I do not desire that this continues, but there are many trite things I could say about it all that would put my whining to shame. Also, how closely this approximates to last month as a cycle is bizarre. On 21 August, 'I' appeared which gives hope for 21 September. I am still preparing everything for the Seven Days and I have begun re-reading *Cosmic Fire* to answer yesterday's questions. Also, in my oration, I am pleading for strength and spirit to see me through. I really need it. Yet I am not confused. I am hanging in darkness between literally (vanity) Heaven and Earth. Yet, spirit is black. In the Song of Solomon: 'I am Black and Comely, oh ye daughters of Jerusalem.' That, I hope, is the answer. My love to all my brothers and sisters.

Operation kept to.

P.S. Frances has just told me that she has had two bad nights. Wot wiv all this and my solar plexus, perhaps I am being deliberately used as a vacuum-cleaner for astral shit, i.e. the Third Demand.

16 September

The most tortuous day yet, but I think/hope it reached a climax at midday. I am (or have) raised the *kundalini* energy through a second hole in my head; I do not think the channel is clear yet. No one, except a brother, can appreciate the psychic and personal pain one goes through, but this has its silver lining as, for instance, it led me today to an actual positive desire to enter a state that has previously been the ultimate in paranoid and hysterical fear. The black energy, the rush of fear of overwhelming darkness, I have pushed towards it – even now a bit nervously – and it has to a degree rushed in, by this new hole in my head(!). The fight is very, very acute and bitter. Perhaps this is Armageddon. (I am brought that concept by Manly P. Hall's *Masonic and Rosicrucian etc. Encyclopaedia* which is a great comfort to me, providing my only literary relaxation. Also today, 'All Gas and Gaiters' on the B.B.C. World Service – a religious comedy show. I must have an ally in Bush House. I mean, *we* must have an ally...) In the Oratory this evening, for the first time, astral figures in my head – enormous Egyptian priests; all very pretty, but not, I think, relevant. This is truly a time of change, I think. I know nothing at all. I know only that I am still – for all these grand energies – a vain selfish worm. What exactly, it struck me today, am I actually doing to send out really good, high, loving energy in my life between praying? Answer: nothing. It must change. For the Lord, the One God, is a Loving God.

Operation kept to.

17 September

Today is different from the preceding cycle from which I am emerging, although I am not in full consciousness. The loving joy which I mentioned yesterday as being what I should emit continuously, is being applied as Law today with painful but worthwhile (surprise surprise) effects. Last night I was faced with a flow of energies (which yesterday I boasted I was now welcoming) and I turned my eyes away again like a nervous dog – but I was frightened. I am still nervous at the concept and, if faced again with it, am uncertain that I can hold my eyes and consciousness steady, though I will to try. I feel somewhat pathetic about that, and about everything else today – like a relatively well-meaning but intrinsically selfish little puppy, with all the images that go with it. All this is strangely unrelated to the Operation – I think. I really am not intellectually or psychically certain about anything. There are, however, sharp energies flowing through my skull and brain. I have not been mentally tranquil today, my brain will-o'-wisping about and I not being strict enough with it – even now, as I write. But, the most beautiful 'thing' in the Oratory at lunchtime (and it was much needed to lift me) showed me that there was now a smile over my head instead of the halo of 2 August. I found that very funny – it was a lovely and much appreciated present. And now I feel guilty that I require this attention to keep me toddling happily along. 'A smile catches the dew of paradise. Always smile.'

Operation kept to.

18 September

A small amount of clear light at the end of the tunnel. I see, perhaps, the end of this razor edge. Joy and bliss wiping out pain is the answer and it is almost here today; almost, as I cannot hold it in my weakness. Buddhic consciousness also returns intermittently today. The thing, though, has been to live it – to live it in the family here. Strange, every time I am what the Master D.K. calls a point of tension, I think that the strained consciousness is only going to get weirder until I manage to accustom myself; whereas the truth is always that 'one returns to the calm of where one was', but with a *new* dimension which, I think, pushes an earlier dimension below the threshold of consciousness. I feel slightly calmer about the end of the Operation. I have not broken any of the rules. I am afraid now of the Angels and God and not of anything else. I fear to insult them with my grossness and ignorance. I am in their most beautiful hands and my thought and wish is that it will be the most amazing Grace, of which I am not worthy.

Operation kept to.

I very nearly forgot to write this. Yesterday and today I was quite overcome by the miracle of (as H.C.A. said in a letter yesterday) getting off the lavatory and arriving in and being in La Vallée Heureuse *(i.e. leaving the city and coming to this glorious valley in the mountains.)*. Truly, some tears. And today, we suddenly remember, is the anniversary of that levitation.

(A further ten minutes later) It strikes me, therefore, that it is a most auspicious time indeed. The beginning of a journey? But tonight there was a sudden and huge flow of egocentricity which shames me and is the last one ever for me. God, what a pathetic wreck I am, yet tonight I nevertheless feel a joy. And a speed. Mmm.

19 September

A day of acute energies and great weirdness. I am (or I have put myself) under great and tremendous strain. I am finding it somewhat difficult even to write this. Perhaps it is a final all-out manoeuvre to stop me; if so, far too late. Perhaps it is a reappearance – but for the absolutely final encore – of my personality which is trying to shriek at the strain and slide out of this glorious commitment; if so, again, *far* too late. It is at this point that I become truly the warrior, Christ's Knight for myself, for my brothers and sisters, but most for His glory (though He hardly has any need of me, no matter how much I understand the coming of the Fifth Kingdom and the other 'esoteric' teaching concerning evolution). In the Oratory this evening, sparks of white light and even some electric crackling noises (like two wires being brushed against each other); the duality in my head (between ajna *(forehead)* and throat/mouth, it feels) most extreme and observable. An annoying attack and threat which, as I left the Oratory, turned out to be only six inches high! Truly, though, the point of tension is acutely high. My feelings about the end of the Operation are confused; a prince among men, a worm among Angels. I will be frightened; I will insult Them with my ignorance, arrogance, grossness; I will insult His wisdom with my vanity, slowness... And then remembering how we have been brought here. And if I occasionally have fearful doubts about this being 'a real thing', I only have to think to my physical head which is still under great internal pressure, and its whole shape has changed, though my hair now growing, disguises it. What trivia! But everything that we know – everything! – is trivia in comparison to a grain of the understanding and glory...

Again, as last night, as I write this diary, the energy coming through is quite shamingly and childishly apparent. I would only make one thing clear – that this is not a crisis on the level of the Fourth Kingdom. Brezhnev, Nixon, Amin and Kaddafi could walk together and without warning into this house and leave, I hope, better and happier men. Oi! True. The crisis is elsewhere and it is in the knowledge of my total weakness and ignorance and sheer clumsiness that I fear and am nervous. What else can I say? My trust also is elsewhere, is it not? Above, unto the God the One God Our Lord and His servants who deign to order and lead and guard me. So all praise unto the One. All praise. As this century turns, we shall see His Kingdom come. Truly.

Operation kept to. Again, the duality is severe and amusing. I – I might only smile on. It is very difficult today. Mmm? The truth of the matter is that I am in a highly-tuned state of anticipation and this is causing (or is coincident to) a vast flow of energies through me. I also take into account the flashings which I have not previously experienced. Yes?

20 September
(4.30 pm) Everything is ready. I stop writing for a minute as duality flashes through and I watch these hands with the biro – for the Consecration is tomorrow; and I cannot put myself into a calm and

glowing state – nor do I know if I am supposed to. It would, I think, be a strange initiate who was not nervous and the instruction is clear *and* unavoidable that one must humiliate oneself with fervour. It is my ardent wish for future travellers of this path that the route to communication with the Higher Hierarchies should be less personally tortuous and more (intellectually and socially) straightforward. Perhaps when the Mystery Schools are reinstated this will become a reality. I have a small ulcer in the right-hand side of my mouth, as opposed to the left where one has been in the past – no doubt this is progress. I am fluid enough for spots to have appeared on my face (though perhaps that is due to not washing my newly-grown hair thoroughly enough).

I suppose that the element which makes for the greatest tension and the most 'weirdness' is that I have never met anyone in the flesh who would relate to or, more importantly, be able intelligently to educate me in these matters. The books say it all. But, again, it is my ardent wish that the Mysteries *(the esoteric and magical teachings)* become sufficiently exoteric *(public)* to make it unnecessary for this kind of track to be walked in this sort of darkness. Though I am here, what! When the men on our planet have had the material glamour lifted from their eyes, they will see. For instance, to assume that the divine voice in the back of one's head, guiding and braking, is created by grey oozing flesh that is the brain – a gross flabby organ – is sufficient to show the heavy thickness of the veil that blinds the most intelligent of men. But we – the disciples, aspirants and children – will dissolve and remove that veil. And therefore the Kingdom of God is obviously on its way.

Having reassured myself on that – and you, my brother – I have filled some fifteen minutes and must find something correct to do. Ah, the duality is most interesting as both parts are agreed on one great topic – their horribleness before God and His Angels. An inability from either side to be anything but clumsy. I AM (sneer, sneer) THAT I AM (snivel, snivel). I may only add that I am neither feeling nor behaving very well, but that inane grin is shining again which also shames me. There is no way out of my wormhood.

(9.00 pm) Well, the six months are over – the Six Moons of Preparation – and it is a miracle to me in all ways. In one way I would have them go on and on, for it is a purificatory process and I am not pure. Whatever the outcome of next week, that I *will* continue. I so swear. Frances today said that she would not look at the toads if she did not like them; which is pertinent to what I feel

about the Angel's attitude towards me. Between writing this today, I felt a charge within, telling me to relax, making me relax. I find it difficult. There is little to write now. All the notes concerning the Seven Days are in a separate notebook. I have been weeping much today in shame. My trust is in His Mercy and Justice which are ever correct.

Operation kept to!

The Seven Days of Consecration, Convocation and Conjuration

Day of Consecration

When first ye shall enter into the Oratory, leave your shoes without, and having opened the window, ye shall place the lighted coals in the Censer which you shall have brought with you, you shall light the lamp, and take from the Cupboard of the Altar your two vestments, the Crown, the Girdle and the Wand, placing them upon the Altar. Then take the Sacred Oil in your left hand, cast some of the Perfume upon the Fire, and place yourself upon your knees, praying unto the Lord with fervour...

Having finished your Orison, rise from your knees, and anoint the centre of your forehead with a little of the Sacred Oil; after this dip your finger into the same Oil, and anoint therewith the four corners of the Altar. Touch also with this Holy Oil the Vestments, the Girdle, the Crown, and the Wand, on both sides. You shall also touch the Doors and the Windows of the Oratory. Then with your finger dipped in the Oil you shall write upon the four sides of the Altar these words, so that they may be perfectly clearly written on each side:

"In whatever place it may be wherein Commemoration of My Name shall be made, I will come unto you and I will bless you."

From the instructions of the Sacred Magic
(See pages 78-80 of the facsimile.)

21 September

(9 am) Rose at 5.30 and made the consecration, coming out of the Oratory at 7 am The weather has suddenly turned cold. If I be sufficiently purified for tomorrow, then it is the spirit of the Lord and not by virtue of my own merit or effort. I stumble and am clumsy, even in the consecration. (I meant to note yesterday that I have been consulting the *I Ching* daily and he has been advising me perfectly. If I am so graced as to bring this Operation unto a successful conclusion, then I shall find out who is responsible for the Changes (I mean the dynamics of the *I Ching*) and I will thank and thank him for his continual consideration.)

I pray again at midday and twilight; though the instructions are not crystal clear from Abraham, I take it to be so and have intuited no contradiction. It was, I must say, very glorious to see everything on the altar and to smell the oil.

(9 pm) After an unpleasantly intense and very shaming day, the atmosphere has suddenly eased this evening. If, however, I were to concentrate on what is happening, I would shamefully collapse in tears again. I have begged today that I should die. *(I meant that my personality should die.)* And that is a strange thing, perhaps, that even now I think always towards Initiation. Perhaps this is only because, in reality, I cannot stretch my intellect to conceive of what, God willing, is about to take place.

I have been reading the biography of *Milarepa* which I find most comforting. I see from a note concerning raising the *kundalini* energy that my Teacher has indeed been closer than I imagined. It is only now that I begin to see certain truths and my future here must depend on what I learn that I must do to perfect and liberate myself; or what I am told to do. I *am* His servant, whether accepted or not. There is, however and *perhaps*, a change happening. May He give me strength and grace for the next few days.

Day One completed – The Day of Consecration.

First Day of the Convocation of the Angels

 ake a Robe of Mourning; enter the Oratory with bare feet; go unto the side of the Censer, take the ashes therefrom and place them upon your head... Humiliate yourself before God and His Celestial Court, and commence your prayer with fervour, for then it is that you will begin to enflame yourself in praying, and you will see appear an extraordinary and supernatural Splendour which will fill the whole apartment, and will surround you with an inexpressible odour, and this alone will console and comfort your heart so that you shall call for ever happy the Day of the Lord."

From the instructions of the Sacred Magic
(See pages 81-85 of the facsimile.)

22 September
(9.45 am) I cannot say. I do not know what has (not) happened. I am, however, in a different psychic space. I do not know. 'The Lord will perfect that which concerneth me.' If He so wills.

Day Two, the First Day of the Convocation of the Angels.

Second Day of the Convocation of the Angels

 nd thus shall ye pray unto the utmost degree that shall be possible unto you, and with the greatest fervour... During the space of two or three hours. Then quit the Oratory, returning thither at midday for another hour, and equally again in the evening... Understand also that the odour and the splendour will in nowise quit the Oratory."

From the instructions of the Sacred Magic
(See pages 81-85 of the facsimile.)

23 September
(3 pm) Again, I cannot say. I dare not and I cannot. As Abraham says, tomorrow is when the Operator will first be able to see if he has well used the previous six months unto the service of God. Whatever does – or does not – happen, my concern will be to know, to learn how I may liberate myself in *this* lifetime, may reintegrate in this lightning life. The biography of Milarepa much cheered me

– and how pleasant that I should read it now; and know that my aspiration is *not* impossible. To renounce fully in the twentieth century is the same but different from the eleventh century and those times; now, it must be done within the mind, and even while living a material life one's whole aspiration and spiritual desire must be to the Reality. To eke out a living, yet not care. It is very difficult. Only do I praise fate and the Gods and the Angels that eighteen months ago, when I pledged myself to a total break, circumstances were with us – or to be exact, before I went broke we left with enough to scrape through the time to fulfil this Operation. Over the last six months I have consciously learnt many things– some of which I knew before, but did not know were the privilege (or pain) of initiates, others of which I could not even have dreamed and even now stretch my pathetic mind as I attempt clumsily to understand. And even then, all that...

(What happened to me on the day of the full invocation of my Guardian Angel was so terrible and incomprehensible that a couple of days later I tore out the page in my hand-written diary which linked the 23rd to the 24th September; I tore it out and burned it. Where I tore it out, I wrote in the diary: 'Here I have torn out a page as it contained things I feel happier not being in this diary and therefore able to be read by someone else who may perform this Operation.' I will explain below why I tore it out.)

Third Day of the Convocation of the Angels

lace yourself on your knees before the Altar, to render thanks to God for His benefits, and firstly for having granted unto you a treasure so great and so precious. You shall render thanks also unto the Holy Guardian Angels, praying unto them that henceforward they will have you in their care... And then shall you first be able to put to the test whether you shall have well employed the period of your Six Moons, and how well and worthily you shall have laboured in the quest of the Wisdom of the Lord; since you shall see your Guardian Angel appear unto you in unequalled beauty... Observe that on the third day you should remain in familiar conversation with your Guardian Angel."

From the instructions of the Sacred Magic
(See pages 81-85 of the facsimile.)

24 September

(The diary continues) ...It is not, I find, quite possible to put into clear writing what I felt at that moment – or what I feel now. If only one thing, it has proved that I am psychically indestructible (God willing). Only shall I say that I myself have been a scream of pain and loss that never ends. At the time, the most acute thought was that I must give up everything and go to a monastery; only then shall I find the jewel that I yearn for. So clearly answering came a voice within, defiantly screaming against it, clinging to everything.

I, in a total daze, left the Oratory and fell into bed; I wished not to think or to be conscious. My dream was filled with evil things ending with a humiliating ploy which led me to ejaculate.

It is also worth noting that on Friday night, in bed, such a charge of thrilling electric energy was passed through my body that I, in total reflex action, ejaculated also; at the time, I was not shamed; this morning I am. (How strangely material that sex – 'a short word used for a long long topic', as the Master D.K. says – should appear here. It is *not* relevant but I must write down the truth.)

And now? This moment, I am in total limbo. (Frances' dog has disappeared, presumably dead, and that is a very tortuous situation for her to deal with objectively.) Where and what am I? Where must I now go and what must I do? How high (or low!) am I initiated? Just how blind or vain have I been – am I still? Am I not what I thought I was? Is all that only fantasy?

To what sort of a life should I now go? The idea of a monastery causes me pain in many ways; perhaps that is exactly why it has to be done. Rather a slum room in the city and to care for the street children; a form of activity. Is praying all the time a form of arrogance? Am I allowed a personal future? *What* am I now to do?

For the moment I know only that I *must*, whatever, keep on praying and praising God. I feel temptations all around me – I resist them. Only do I beg to be allowed out of this confusion. Always in the past these climaxes have heralded a new clarity. I am nervous now of the vision ahead; I cannot in any way see it.

(1 pm) What an amazing fool I am. Having written the above, I returned to the Oratory to pray and my Teacher talked with me. All becomes clear.

(4.45 pm) Everything occurs as Abraham wrote. I have full conversation with my Holy Guardian Angel.

(7.15 pm) This is definitely the last entry for today. All is now

calmer; to be exact, I am calm. Everything is clear concerning the conjurations; my Guardian Angel who is holy and righteous, making me a worm but ever trying to elevate me (which makes me see much: e.g., before Him, my body was as ugly and uncontrolled as the effect that I sometimes have on others), has made everything clear. About this morning, I am not understanding. Nothing spiritual or psychic could ever throw me back now; perhaps it was a method whereby I finally fully relinquished the hold of my (dearly beloved) intellect and put myself totally into His hands.

Frances' little doggy came back ten minutes ago, teaching her many things. And a letter was received today from W.A. who wishes desperately to understand, and he is more than able; this made me very happy. A year ago we left Europe. This week shall always be sacred to me. I prepare now for tomorrow morning and beg His continued Virtue, Grace and Force.

Day Four, the Third Day of the Convocation of the Angels.

I must now put my head permanently into that graceful state that I may enjoy His conversation. He told me that is how He would ever see me. I have found my Elder Brother; He has deigned to find and care for me. May I never shame myself before Him.

My Angel made me shuffle and twitch. All Glory to Him.

I shall finally mention that my doubts as to whether it was a real thing or not were totally cut by many things, but three mainly:

1.   That He explained to me the rebellion of Angels that made these spirits punished by God and sentenced to serve me and other men;

2.   I threw the Ching asking for 'Youthful Folly' and received it;

3.   Finally that, as I say, He made me shuffle and be clumsy in His presence.

(I finally had full and complete conversation with this great angelic being and consciousness. So what had happened to me in the Oratory?

When this diary was originally published in 1976, I did not write an explanation of what had happened in the Oratory. I did not write such an explanation for two reasons. First, I thought that what happened to me, which had caused me awful distress, was a final test for all magicians attempting to complete the Abramelin ritual. This was the main reason why I tore out the relevant page, in case it fell into the hands of a future candidate for this ceremony. I also did not really understand what had happened.

Fifteen years later, however, teaching one of my Angel courses at the Findhorn Foundation I finally understood what had, in fact, happened.

I went into the Oratory to make my final prayer asking for communication with my Holy Guardian Angel and then to await its presence. I said the prayer with all the fire and devotion that were the climax of the six months preparation. Those moments held all my expectation. They held the totality of my psychic, psychological and physical investment – all the accumulated time and energy from the moment that I had first decided to perform this ritual. I completed my prayer and on my knees, my head bowed in abject humility, my body bent in taut tension, my whole being thrust forward awaiting the visitation, nothing happened. I waited and there was nothing. I waited some more and still there was nothing.

I came out of my state of intense prayer and invocation, and came into a new awareness, an awareness purely of myself. My psyche turned ice cold in frigid self-consciousness. I looked coldly at myself. I was alone and my own witness. I saw myself enveloped in all the physical and psychic paraphernalia of the ceremony: the robes, the lamp, the incense, the altar, my bent body, all the time and intensity... And nothing was now happening.

I had launched myself into a vacuum.

In those minutes I, the witness to myself, was both cynic and vanquished. There were many thoughts, but most of all a sense of everything having been stripped away and I was left with nothing but the appearance. There was nothing but form and appearance. The materialists were right. This was all there was. Everything else, mystic and divine, was of the pathetic human imagination. I had been lost in pathetic fantasy and delusion.

Yet, as I thought all that, I was also simultaneously the mystic and magician, but I was the magician who had been completely vanquished. I had tried my best but, in this final judgement, had been found worthless, no scraps of divine insight to be thrown to me. I, who had for so long recognised myself as worm – at least in my orations – was truly worm, lost and loser.

I put out the oil lamp and walked back into the house. Frances asked how it all was and I did not answer, barely acknowledging her, putting on the false front of a man walking as if on important business. I entered the bedroom and collapsed on the bed, my hands and arms protecting and comforting my head. I breathed for a while in deep and incomprehensible gasps. Then, for a while, there were tears but no deep sobs. I fell into a fitful sleep and was woken by the embarrassment of an uncontrolled electric ejaculation. But I had become more calm. And then I heard a sweet and beautiful voice in my head. "Come back into the Oratory. Come back into the Oratory."

I nodded, stood and walked back to the Oratory where I lit the lamp and knelt again before the altar. I felt this presence around me and it spoke clearly to me, telling me it was my Guardian Angel sent by God to be with me and to protect me and to help me. It told me that it loved me with all the love of the most devoted parent, brother and friend, and that I would never be alone again.

What I had not understood then, but understood later in that workshop at Findhorn, was why it was necessary for me to leave the Oratory and then return. Nowadays, when I teach people how to perceive and attune to other presences, such as the angelic, I try to help them reach a state of carefully focused attention whilst at the same time staying perfectly relaxed and playful so that they can be open to impression. To perceive these other realities, to be fully open to understanding one's intuitive sensitivity, we need to be focused but relaxed. In the oratory that day, I was in such a state of intense focus and concentration that I had lost that calm, relaxed receptive state which is a prerequisite for angelic attunement. I remember myself screwed up before the altar, a ball of fiery concentration, eyes screwed tight, brow intensely furrowed. In the release that followed in the bedroom my terrible tension relaxed. Once I was calm and 'open' again, the Angel could communicate to me.)

First Day of Conjuration

ou shall then robe yourself, taking first the White Vestment, and over this you shall put on that of Silk and Gold, then the Girdle, and upon your head you shall place the Crown, and you shall lay the Wand upon the Altar... you shall take your Wand in your right hand, and pray unto God to give unto this Wand as much virtue, force and power as He gave unto those of Moses, of Aaron, of Elijah, and of the other Prophets whose number is infinite.

Now place yourself beside the Altar looking towards the Door and the open Terrace; or if you be in the Country place yourself at the Western side, and commence by summoning the Chief Spirits and Princes... Make each one of them touch the Wand and take the Oath upon that Wand."

From the instructions of the Sacred Magic
(See pages 86-103 of the facsimile.)

25 September

(11.30 am) I rose at 5.30 and entered the Oratory at ten minutes to six, and I changed into my Magician's vestments. It had taken me some time to get to sleep last night, my mind racing on W.A. and my pleasure at his demand *(A letter from a friend asking for spiritual advice)*, but I had slept soundly from midnight. I was slightly nervous, but the amusing and saving point was/is that mental part of me that was frightened was also the same part that said this was all no real thing – how, therefore, could I have it both ways?

Having robed myself, I fell to my knees and prayed as directed in the Book and, naturally, by my heart. I shortly felt my Angel's presence and heard his words. How amazing yet natural to write all this... I stood, wand in my right hand and Psalm XIC in my left hand, and called the four princes. Within a few minutes they came, only twice attempting to frighten me, once with a great whooshing sound that burnt my back (and the little doggy came past) and later pretending they were behind and threatening me. And then they did each take the correct oath. The marvel was that my Angel had so well prepared me over the last six months that the whole thing was done with the most great and surprising ease. He had made me so that my attitude was almost impeccable and the four princes knew it was not worth their while to chide or insult or seek to ensnare me. Psalm XIC holds great mysteries that gave me much strength and understanding. Though I was to constrain the four princes to appear in the shape of men, they took no shape and for a while this confused me. I looked to my Angel for explanation and confirmation, and he told me that, as I knew, they were not of gross matter and if they appeared in a human shape, it would only be one of a cliché pulled from kama-manasic matter of which I had no need. My faith was sufficient and I was also too sophisticated, thanks to what I had learned from the Tibetan's books, to need all that visualisation to make it a real thing.

There was also an amusing side to the whole affair in that it seemed to me again that the whole valley was filled with specta-tors – Spectators – as though at a boxing-match; and at one point when one of the princes was reluctant concerning his oath, the crowd shouted for him to take it, *all* the Members of the Assembly being on my side as though supporting David against Goliath; the prince did quickly swear.

Thus was it all exactly as Abraham wrote it. And my most beautiful beloved Angel had so well taught me that it was all easy. What can I, in words, say or add about it? I now prepare for tomorrow.

Last night great floods of energy were again passed through me. My skull, as ever, is still under great internal pressure and changing shape. I have an unsubstantiated theory that in order for one's higher mental senses and intuitions to be brought into activity, actual physical pressure must be taken off the appropriate lobes of the brain; obviously(?) the only way to do this is to enlarge the cranium which is, in fact, what has been occurring with me. This must, I think, needs be so that all my communication with the Angels and spirits – with the members of the sub- or super-human Hierarchies – is done on that high intuitive level; which is amazingly fast and acute compared to the normal lumbering mental actions of the brain. All the conscious intellect must do is trust in the reality of this new form of communication and realize how crippled it has previously been. At all of this am I but a stumbling beginner and I must learn these new rules and methods.

All that has happened today, has happened *only* by the Grace, Favour and Force of God. It has nothing to do with my own virtue which *is* negligible. It is no great thing (though admittedly rare nowadays) to put one's trust in God – and that only means to recognize the *real* Truths, to be prepared to transmute the shit that is oneself into gold – *but it is a great thing that having put one's trust in Him He should then so favour one.* In time this will be so for *all* men. Brothers like myself will not be the exception.

When a man first walks off dry land which is solid and holding him firmly, into water, he must trust that the water will also hold him, but in a different fashion from solidly and firmly. The man, as we all know, who does not have this trust will never be able to swim. Frightened, nervous children must be led and taught lovingly. There must be no fear of anything. I feel, and this is the miracle, that I am being lovingly taught with tolerance and great goodness. Ah, but I dare to say that I *plunged* in on my own and am, therefore, receiving this teaching. There are levels. I now lose myself in words that cannot express, that I cannot clarify, which show that ever before Him I am a worm.

I look forward now to slowing down.

(5.30 pm) Having just been in the Oratory to collect the ashes and prepare the lamp, I am reminded that I should have mentioned that the four princes left marks on the sand – surprisingly and funnily, this startles me. It is a real thing.

This afternoon I became involved in trying to loosen Frances' personality from her soul and was greatly provoked – this follows *(the metaphorical advice concerning)* taking a maiden to wife from the

Ching (and I had been strangely depressed. I am like a clumsy impatient child for the Jewel of the Philosophers, whatever this Operation. This altogether raises another point of two realities and problems of orientation and crass donkey-like blindness.) Anyway, the whole fandango with the lady caused pain and heavily was I then menaced by Belial (the perfidious!). *(It felt as if one of the daemonic beings surfaced as if called by my bad mood. This was indeed true and I learnt quickly that I could not even consider certain attitudes and moods as they conjured up those energies whom I needed to control and not have as co-creating colleagues.)* The Angel then spoke to me, echoing my own words that now I must be for every minute the Knight, the Cavalier – if not, look what I lay myself open to. *Whatever* the provocation, with these odds, there seems little choice. Depression *is* dangerous; it used to be very painful. This is perhaps an interesting bit (gulp) of helpful blackmail – to see me through the next two days or over another hurdle – or the same thing.

Ever up on the spiral one is confronted with one's childishness and yet again one is – I am – shamed.

Day Five, the First Day of the Conjuration of the Evil Spirits: Lucifer, Satan, Belial and Leviathan.

All Glory to the One.

Second Day of Conjuration

26 September

(8.30 am) This morning, I with great ease (and with much help) conjured, constrained and made take the appropriate oaths, the eight sub-princes. Last night, however, I was extremely frightened. I must now begin to restrict what I am to say. As one progresses along the Path, there are certain 'tests and tribulations' and it would not be correct for a fellow-aspirant (a dear and loved brother) to be forewarned. And I am worried lest this diary should be lost or I may at some point wish a friend or brother to read it. It is only completely true that a *complete trust* in God and the Hierarchy will see one through everything.

Last night my human Teacher made himself fully known to me. He is the Master R. What I wrote yesterday concerning that control (under a threat of blackmail) is correct; and that will take me forward. Not surprisingly, I am assimilating, considering, synthesizing. The biggest thing is to trust, trust, trust and be in that noble knowing space. W.A. makes me still very happy and I am laying plans for him.

Third Day of Conjuration

27 September

(11 am) This morning I successfully completed the conjuration and took all the required oaths. I was not feeling physically well and at one point thought that I was not going to be able to endure and hold together until the end. I was a whole sixty minutes or so constraining them, though with the help of my Angel and the Audience it was, in fact, smoothly easy; though the spirits – the servitors – were more unruly than the princes were yesterday and the day before. Two of the familiars were also somewhat rebellious and cunning, but they soon behaved once correctly threatened. I did, however, make one gaff. With groups two to eight (of the twelve, the ones marked on the separate list) I forgot to propound to them the section concerning any new symbols I might care to make or use; and so I pulled all eight of these groups together at the same time to remind them. It is technically interesting that if I focused too hard on seeing them and talking to them through my ajna centre, I felt a great electric gnawing at my forehead which I could not at the time endure for longer than ten seconds. As it is this black 'gnawing' that used to give me the screaming heeby-jeebies, I am not dismayed.

I now give thanks for seven days, starting from tomorrow, and, also starting tomorrow, I fast for three days before putting the Operation to work. Abraham's advice is to remember that one is first an apprentice and only later a master, and so I shall take my time in learning this Art. Truly is it a (I note the medieval style!) miracle: the whole thing, especially that for six months *nothing* went wrong. For that, thanks. And with some sophistication now – though I am still learning its truth – do I say that Trust is a most marvellous thing.

EPILOGUE

And so the ceremony came to a successful conclusion. I was not then capable of stopping to gather myself. I could not pause to reflect upon all that happened. I was incapable of reflection. I was still caught in the dynamic psychic velocity of concentration and wilfulness that had taken me into the operation in the first place and then seen me through it. I simply could not be calm and reflective. My mind and my psyche were throbbing with the intensity and the exertion. The terrible duality that I mentioned so often in the diary continued in the days following the completion.

On the one hand I had taken my consciousness through into new dimensions and had experienced, and still was experiencing, an ongoing bliss and cosmic consciousness. I had also fully opened the doors of my perception on to the angelic realm. I could now openly perceive and enter into telepathic rapport with this whole parallel dimension. But, although open to these transcendent realities, although now in continuous mystical communion with the transcendent, my personality and my psyche were still running on an intense, even manic, rhythm.

On one hand I was the disciplined and opened mystic. On the other I was still the extreme personality who had forced my spiritual way forward. This is a not uncommon spiritual pattern, often romantically described as 'storming heaven.' Reflect, though, on the character traits which are needed for such an assault. Having stormed heaven, these traits themselves need to be transformed. Many mystics, especially those filled with fiery aspiration, tend towards craziness. Many gurus and mystical teachers have uncontrollable personality traits left over from the dynamics that took them through their spiritual changes in the first place.

So... I had completed the great ceremony. I had achieved the Conversation. I had opened my mystical awareness. But I still had that whole complex of personality characteristics needing transformation, exacerbated now by the intensity of the six month process and by the new awarenesses and energies. I remember my feelings: Attention! Let me fulfil my duty! Let me save and resurrect things! Let me express my avataric Mission! On duty! To work!

But an extraordinary process of healing and further transformation, in a completely unexpected guise, was about to take place.

Frances, thoroughly exhausted by the six months, immediately took a three week break in London, leaving me on my own, and a few days after her departure I fell very ill. On her return, at her insistence and at the urgings of some neighbours who were by now despairing of the colour I had turned, I visited a French doctor in Marrakesh who informed me that I had a severe case of Hepatitis-B. I was so ill that he offered me a bed in his own home and he intimated that my case had progressed so far that it might not turn around.

We stayed up in the mountains and finally I collapsed completely. I was on my back for several months, so weak that I was virtually unable to move. On several occasions I enjoyed, in full consciousness, the classic near-death experience of being out of my body and part of a decision-making process concerning whether I would live. I found these experiences extremely beautiful and deeply reassuring; death is now a trusted and loving friend for me. The illness and convalescence lasted almost two years. Two years with no energy. Many months on my back. For some of the time my blood was so badly oxygenated that my brain functioned at a tenth of its normal speed. Someone would say something to me; it would take me two minutes to process the words, understand them and then come up with a reply; by which time the speaker had moved on. I was so ill that I was neither able to reflect on the ceremony nor able to experiment with its effects. In the Summer of 1974 we closed up house and Frances drove us up to Tangier where we took the ferry back to England and where my convalescence continued for another twelve months.

What a wonderful and extraordinary illness it was. How carefully my own soul or my Teacher must have planned it. Twenty years later I can still think of no more efficient or economic way of integrating my energies. How else could I have calmed my psychic explosion and transformed my storming heaven pattern? For two blessed years I had no energy to run my speed or my compulsive personality. I was finally learning what it felt like to be relaxed and simply to be present with no action and no thoughts. I began at last to settle down into the awarenesses I had reached over the six months of the ceremony.

But I need to make clear that the settling down and the integration have been a long and difficult process which lasted well beyond the illness and which only now, almost twenty years later, do I feel nearing completion. This process has included: the grounding and heart-opening that comes from being a parent; a consistent daily rhythm of silence and meditation; the development of mental patience through doing undergraduate and post-graduate study in social theory and psychology; the development of emotional nurture and personality calm through nine years of working with adults and teenagers with special needs; teaching and lecturing about magic and meditation, and attempting to do this teaching in a sensible and integrated way; attempting as a daily practise to be open to honesty, love and transformation. Most of all I do not want to give the impression that the Abramelin Operation was a spiritual event complete in its own timing. It was a way of breaking through into another world, a world of spirit which has since called me ever into deeper exploration.

In the years following the Operation I changed so much that I was no longer the creature who had attracted and interested Frances; and I did not have the skills or the capacity to love her in a way that compensated for my changes. The chemistry she and I had was gone and we were left, two new people, two strangers to each other. Sadly, we separated in 1978, but there was a liberation in it which we both recognised and respected. I look back on that period in Morocco with deep gratitude to her; for I do not know that on my own I would have had the courage to do the ceremony and she certainly had the courage to be there supporting me and dealing with the dynamics, inner and outer, of the whole intense situation. Two decades later our friendship is such that she is the publisher of the book you hold now in your hands.

Having opened the doors on to the angelic realms my interest in that field has expanded and my logical left brain has remained sufficiently active that a few years ago I wrote a study paper for the Findhorn Foundation analysing the nature and purpose of the angelic realm. (*Devas, Fairies and Angels*, Gothic Image, 1990.) And I begin every day by lighting a candle to the Angel of the landscape or the city where I wake up. The angelic realms are a living and relevant reality to me.

Some readers will probably want to know if I ever took advantage of the so-called magical powers available at the completion of the ceremony and I can simply answer that they never interested me. I thought about them for a few days immediately following the ceremony's completion, but I then fell ill and since then they have never tempted me. In the western mystery tradition a clear distinction is made between low and high magic. Low magic is concerned with effects and phenomena; high magic is concerned with using the spiritual 'technology' of magic in order to transform the dross of one's personality into the pure gold of spirit so that one can better serve the Sacred and one's fellow beings. The high magic, also known as the Royal Path of Magic, has interested me, not the phenomena.

I do, however, make use of my skills for cleansing certain situations. But I made a clear decision years ago – lest I be inundated with requests – not to be generally available for individual help. Most individuals who think they might be under attack from occult energies usually need simply either to calm themselves and disengage from a false drama, or else to cleanse and purify their life style for a while. Speaking from experience, I am also of very little help with people diagnosed as schizophrenic or manic depressive; I wish I were, but I am not. I do, however, run occasional trainings in magical work and people who are interested can write to me, care of the publisher.

There are other readers who might wonder if I would recommend the ceremony to others. For a while I described the Abramelin Ceremony as a 'Piscean way of how not to do it,' because it is an extreme technique, belonging to a culture of wilful sacrifice and humbling devotion, which I associated with patriarchal modes that I did not feel appropriate for our emerging non-sexist and holistic spiritual culture. Recently, however, I have begun to feel warmer towards it and perhaps the ritual is still appropriate for some folk. It obviously, however, requires a certain psychological strength. If you do consider it, I must advise you to be very careful and realistic about your psychological capabilities and limits; even the well-known occultist, Aleister Crowley, knew his limits and never performed the Abramelin Ceremony except as a self-confessed exercise in his imagination. If you have any doubts do not even consider it. There are many, many paths — and each of us has our own unique way.

What I do find valuable in the Abramelin Ceremony is its necessity for self-discipline. I am happy to be aligned with the emerging spiritual culture known as 'new age' and I am enthusiastic about every individual having the right to choose and create their own spiritual path. But we need to be careful that, in disengaging from the classical paths of spiritual approach, we do not also lose the skills that are essential for travelling the path.

The word 'discipline' has an uncomfortable ring about it in the late twentieth century; it tones of meaningless authority and obedience. But without discipline, any aspiration for spiritual and personal transformation is doomed. It is not simply that love and self-reflection need to be balanced by discipline; it is the fact that love and self-reflection actively require discipline in order to be practised. To love and to be truthful towards oneself require great self discipline.

Equally, there are times when transformation requires no further insights or healing; we simply need to get on with the change and do it. Self-discipline is the fuel for such action. I am not here talking about an ignorant attitude that represses pain or ignores the necessity of healing. I am only echoing what has *always* been taught by the many different spiritual schools. Forgive the repetition: Love, compassion, service and transformation– they actively require self-discipline in order to be practised.

To conclude, what in essence would I like readers to take away from this book? It is, I suppose, this:

The world into which we are born is overwhelming in its stimulations and apparent necessities. Yet we all of us have an instinct for something deeper, less bound by form. We all of us have an instinct to expand into our real consciousness and to wake up fully to our relationship with this sacred cosmos. The world of form and human society, with its overwhelming stimulations, holds us in deep attraction so that we experience pain as we disengage from it to align with spiritual realities. This inner pain, this fear and anxiety, can prevent us serving and transforming. But if we balance our instinct for love with *spiritual courage*, then we can truly move forward – for ourselves and for all life.

BOOK LIST

Listed below are the books referred to in the text of *The Sacred Magician:*

Alice Bailey,   *A Treatise on Cosmic Fire*
                 A Treatise on White Magic
                 Discipleship in the New Age
                 Esoteric Astrology
                 Esoteric Healing
                 Esoteric Psychology Vol I and II
                 From Bethlehem to Calvary
                 Rays and Initiations All: Lucis Press
Louis Carpentier, *Mysteries of Chartres Cathedral*, Rilko
George Clay (trans), *Hundred Thousand Songs of Milarepa*, Harper
    Torchbooks
W.B.Crow, *History of Witchcraft and Occultism*, Abacus
Aleister Crowley, *Magic in Theory and Practice*, Castle
W.Y. Evans-Wentz, *The Tibetan Book of the Great Liberation*, OUP
W.Y. Evans-Wentz, *Tibet's Great Yogi Milarepa*, OUP
Dion Fortune, *The Cosmic Doctrine*, Helios Books
Dion Fortune, *The Mystical Qabalah*, Benn
Manley Palmer Hall,*The Secret Teachings of All Ages*,
    The Philosophical Research Society
Aldous Huxley, *The Doors of Perception*, Panther
Francis King, *Ritual Magic in England*, Spearman
Timothy Leary, *The Politics of Ecstasy*, Paladin
Eliphas Levi, *History of Magic*, Rider
Eliphas Levi, *Transcendental Magic*, Rider
MacGregor Mathers (ed),*The Sacred Magic of AbraMelin the Mage*,
    Watkins 1898
Pauwels & Bergier, *Morning of the Magicians*, Mayflower
Trevor Ravenscroft, *The Spear of Destiny*, Corgi
Israel Regardie, *The Tree of Life*, Samuel Weiser Inc.
Mouni Sadhu, *The Tarot*, Allen & Unwin
Mouni Sadhu, *Samadhi*, Allen & Unwin
K.Seligmann, *Magic, Supernaturalism and Religion*, Paladin 1975
A.E.Waite, *The Book of Ceremonial Magic*, University Books
Richard Wilhelm (trans), *I Ching* or *Book of Changes*,
    Routledge & Kegan Paul
Colin Wilson, *The Occult*, Mayflower
The Zohar, Soncino Press